Minot Judson Savage

Light on the Cloud

Or Hints of Comfort for Hours of Sorrow

Minot Judson Savage

Light on the Cloud
Or Hints of Comfort for Hours of Sorrow

ISBN/EAN: 9783337269975

Printed in Europe, USA, Canada, Australia, Japan

Cover: Foto ©Lupo / pixelio.de

More available books at **www.hansebooks.com**

"*There is no death: what seems so is transition.*"
                                                LONGFELLOW.

"*'Tis better to have loved and lost
    Than never to have loved at all.*"
                                TENNYSON.

"*Words weaker than your grief would make grief more;
    Yet* SOMETHING *I did wish to say.*"
                                TENNYSON.

Light on the Cloud;

OR,

HINTS OF COMFORT FOR HOURS OF SORROW.

BY

M. J. SAVAGE,

AUTHOR OF "CHRISTIANITY THE SCIENCE OF MANHOOD."

Boston:
LOCKWOOD, BROOKS, & COMPANY,
381 Washington Street.
1876.

FRANKLIN PRESS: RAND, AVERY, & CO.,
BOSTON.

TO THOSE WHO SORROW.

PREFACE.

NEARLY all the matter of this little volume has been in print before. Some of it has been copied many times, and circulated widely. Parts of it have been called for from California and the Mississippi to Maine. From many sources the advice has come, to put it into permanent form. It is now sent forth with no pretension, and making no claims. It indeed aspires to the sacred work of comfort, but only by hints and whispers that would "let Grief be her own mistress still." The author despises perfunctory or official sympathy. He would simply sit down by the side of those whom the cloud overhangs, and by a pressure of the hand, or a word from the heart, help them believe in the light that is above the clouds and

Preface.

stronger than they. He would not claim to *prove* all he has suggested. One may *hope* the sweetest and best things, if only his hope be rational.

As for the verses, if any one thinks they are not worthy to be called poetry, let them be named whatever they may.

The "parts" of the book can be read continuously; or the paragraphs may be taken at random, and without regard to order.

The book contains nothing sectarian.

CONTENTS.

	PAGE
LIGHT ON THE CLOUD	17
RESIGNATION	19

PART FIRST.
THE MYSTERY OF AFFLICTION.

I.	WHY DO WE SUFFER?	21
II.	PRESENT IGNORANCE	23
III.	THE END OF LIFE	25
IV.	LOST BLESSINGS NOT ALL LOST	28
V.	HOW FINISH COMES	29
VI.	BUT WHY ME?	31
VII.	NO LIFE INCOMPLETE	33
VIII.	TWO SIDES OF DYING	35
IX.	THESE HINTS ONLY A STAFF	37

MYSTERY	38
THE PESCADERO PEBBLES	40

Contents.

PART SECOND.
THE MINISTRY OF AFFLICTION.

		PAGE
I.	Good out of Evil	42
II.	Character born of Sorrow	43
III.	Affliction may help or harm	45
IV.	Trouble develops Sympathy	46
V.	Tears cleanse the Vision	48
VI.	The true End of Life	49
VII.	Life a School	50
VIII.	A Parable of Growth	51
IX.	Affliction lifts up the Life	52
X.	Affliction teaches a Noble Discontent	54
XI.	Affliction tests and gives Assurance	56

HE GIVETH HIS BELOVED SLEEP 59
PEACE 61

PART THIRD.
THE DIVINE ALCHEMY.

I.	Can Hard Things be "for Good"?	63
II.	Is a Broken Home "for Good"?	64
III.	Is Loss of Property "for Good"?	66
IV.	Is Lost Health "for Good"?	67
V.	The Problem a dark one	68
VI.	God no God, if not good	69
VII.	What is our "Good"?	70
VIII.	The Condition of the Promise	72
IX.	Who are "them that love God"?	73

Contents.

		PAGE
X.	LIKE CAUSES PRODUCE OPPOSITE RESULTS	74
XI.	EVIL MAY "WORK FOR GOOD"	75
XII.	APPLES GET SWEET ONLY WHEN RIPE	76

LIFE IN DEATH 78
THE DEAD ACORN 80

PART FOURTH.

DEATH A BLESSING.

I.	HARD TO BELIEVE IN DEATH	82
II.	DIFFERENT THOUGHTS OF DEATH	83
III.	DEATH IS NOTHING	85
IV.	DEATH NOT A CURSE	86
V.	DEATH NOT THE RESULT OF SIN	86
VI.	DEATH THE CONDITION OF LIFE	88
VII.	DEATH MERELY A CHANGE OF RESIDENCE	89
VIII.	ENDLESS EARTH-LIFE A CURSE	91
IX.	DEATH THE CONDITION OF HIGHER LIFE	95
X.	DEATH THE WAY TO PERMANENT UNIONS	97

GOING TO SLEEP. 101
LIFE FROM DEATH. 103

PART FIFTH.

WILLING TO LIVE.

I.	WILLING TO DIE, OR TO LIVE?	104
II.	EASY TO BE WILLING TO DIE	104
III.	WILLING TO LIVE ON CONDITION	106

Contents.

		PAGE
IV.	Hard Things of Life	108
V.	Mystery makes it hard	109
VI.	Unsatisfied Loves	111
VII.	Life's Burdens	113
VIII.	Losses make us unreconciled to Life.	115
IX.	Life is worth living	116
X.	Trust reconciles to Life.	116
XI.	Content with each Step as a Step	121
XII.	Success consistent with Loss	122

At Twilight Time 125
Memory 127

PART SIXTH.

HAPPINESS.

I.	The Pleasant Way	129
II.	Religion has been Gloomy	130
III.	Man naturally seeks Happiness	132
IV.	An Unhappy Universe a Failure	132
V.	Pleasure is Life, and Pain is Death	134
VI.	Happiness essential to Best Work	136
VII.	This the Root of Civilization	138
VIII.	Our Right to Happiness limited	139
IX.	Health a Condition of Happiness	142
X.	Appreciation of Common Things	143
XI.	Noble Happiness in Noble Things	146
XII.	The Noble Things endure	148

God made our Lives to be a Song . 150
Hope 152

PART SEVENTH.

HEAVEN.

		PAGE
I.	Where is Heaven?	154
II.	Most Reasonable Thought of Heaven	159
III.	This Idea gives Room	160
IV.	Analogy supports it	161
V.	The Material Universe still ours	162
VI.	What is Heaven?	162
VII.	Heaven is Harmony	163
VIII.	Heaven is Satisfaction	164
IX.	Heaven is Expansion	166
X.	Heaven is Progress	168
XI.	Terms of Admission	170

PROGRESS 172
A. R. C. 174

LIGHT ON THE CLOUD.

LIGHT ON THE CLOUD.

THERE'S never an always cloudless sky,
    There's never a vale so fair,
But over it sometimes shadows lie
    In a chill and songless air.

But never a cloud o'erhung the day,
    And flung its shadows down,
But on its heaven-side gleamed some ray,
    Forming a sunshine crown.

It is dark on only the downward side:
    Though rage the tempest loud,
And scatter its terrors far and wide,
    There's light *upon* the cloud.

And often, when it traileth low,
    Shutting the landscape out,
And only the chilly east-winds blow
    From the foggy seas of doubt,

Light on the Cloud.

There'll come a time, near the setting sun,
    When the joys of life seem few:
A rift will break in the evening dun,
    And the golden light stream through.

And the soul a glorious bridge will make
    Out of the golden bars,
And all its priceless treasures take
    Where shine the eternal stars.

RESIGNATION.

MY Father, thou art strong. Nought can withstand
    The might of thy right arm ; and yet I bleed,
    Blown on and broken like a weakly reed,
Whilst thou couldst stay the tempest with thy hand.

My Father, thou art wise. The universe
    Thou readest simply, as I read a book ;
    Thou knowest what is best, and yet dost look
Unmoved on what my sad heart calls a curse.

My Father, thou art loving. My full heart,
    That breaks with love, is but a little urn,
    Filled at thine infinite fountain ; yet I yearn
O'er sundered lives thou sufferest torn apart.

'Tis mystery all, O Father ! Love and might
    And wisdom in their triple strength seem vain :
    The blessèd God looks down upon my pain,
While I grope onward through the stumbling night.

Light on the Cloud.

But that he does not help shall be my hope;
  He might prevent; he's wise, and he is love:
  Then there is meaning in it, and 'twill prove,
That, where I may not see, 'tis best to grope.

We lead our children by dark ways. We tell
  Them they must trust us, though they cannot
   see.
  For never boy knew manhood, or could be
Persuaded that the tasks of youth were well.

And yet from lessons learned, and tasks well done,
  Is born the noble life and happy days:
  No runner ever yet was crowned with bays,
Who faltered when the strife had just begun.

Then learn we resignation and firm trust:
  Some line of purpose still our life runs through.
  God's days are many, and our sorrows few;
And joy shall blossom yet from out the dust.

PART FIRST.

THE MYSTERY OF AFFLICTION.

I.—WHY DO WE SUFFER?

JOB is sitting in the ashes. Property is gone. Sons are gone. Daughters are gone. Friends come not nigh. The persons he has saved from injustice, and helped in their poverty, have deserted his hour of calamity. But, though children come not back, perhaps he may retrieve his earthly fortunes by skill and management in his affairs. No, all hope of this is cut off; for he is cursed with a disease that precludes labor, or dealing with his fellow-men. Now, if ever, is the time to doubt if there is any God; or, if there is, that he is just; much more, that he is merciful and kind. Job's wife is decidedly of this opinion; for she urges him to give up his nonsensical trust, to "curse God, and die." And surely she had the logic on her side, so far as men could see. That didn't look like the way a father would treat a child. And certainly it seemed a little unreasonable, in the face of such disaster, to look up, and say, "Our Father who is in heaven."

But Job saw another side of the case. "God has given me good. I trusted him then; for he proved himself kind. Now shall I renounce him because I cannot understand how my present condition can be consistent with that goodness? No! I'll wait and see." That is the attitude of faith, — just the same kind of faith you exercise in the character of a tried friend. Something comes up that seems to impugn his trustworthiness; and you say, "No! That don't seem like him. There may be some explanation. I'll wait and see. I won't believe it of him till I have to."

Here stood Job. Here let us stand. His words — "Have I received good, and shall I not receive evil?" — do not explain a thing. It is all dark as ever. It is only a voice in the dark that says, "I cannot see the way of God; but I will not call it wrong until I can see."

This life is walked under a cloud. We came out of shadow; we go into shadow. What it all means no mortal has yet discovered. But we hear a voice out of the cloud, saying to us, "What I do, thou knowest not now; but thou shalt know hereafter." For the sunrise of the hereafter, then, we must wait; but, meantime, there come to us some few faint gleams of dawn. Their dim twilight is just enough to help our faith, and to make us look more hopefully for the morning.

To the question, "Why do we suffer?" several answers the world has offered. The first one is that of Job's friends; and it has been echoed ever since: "You are worse than others, and are being punished." Christ, both by his words and by his cross, on which he the Perfect groaned and died, has authorized us to deny this. Not that God does not punish for sin, but only that the fact that we suffer is no proof of our sin. Another answer is a denial of Providence, and a reference of all things to unyielding law. This, pushed too far, takes away our God. God is a Providence; and law is wielded by love.

But the question comes back, "Why suffer, then, if the Father of our Lord Jesus Christ be God? He is wise, and knows what is best. He is strong, and can do his will. He is loving, and wishes us no harm. Why, then, pain and loss and weeping?" Just this is the cloud. It does obscure the sun: let us not deny this. But it has rifts and chinks in it, and the rays drop through. At these rays let us look, and see what hints they can give us of the light that is above.

II. — PRESENT IGNORANCE.

It may be necessary in the nature of things, and needful for our highest culture, that we should not know now.

Present ignorance of many of life's problems is natural and necessary. Our earthly existence is a state of tutelage and training. All things can be understood only by the Infinite. Every step of progress is simply the solution of a new problem. Like the schoolboy's advance from simple addition to cube root, it is the mastery of a new principle, the working-out of one more difficulty.

God does not make us walk in darkness for the mere purpose of perplexing us, or to assert his sovereign right to do as he pleases with us. Many of these things we have not yet grown to, and cannot comprehend. Why it is better for a boy to be put to a hard trade, or set to learning the dry formulas of grammar, rather than to be permitted to play through all the long days in the sunshine, is a question that I presume has never yet been made clear to the boyish mind. And it is not parental tyranny nor wilfulness that keeps it a mystery. The boy cannot understand it; for he cannot comprehend the relation of the trade or the grammar to the successes or failures of a life that lies all untried and unknown before him. Present ignorance is needful to the development in us of some of the highest graces of character.

If a child should say about father or mother, "I'll believe in them just so far as I can keep my eye on facts, and no farther," you would say, "Either those are very unworthy parents, or that is a very unworthy child." If parents are not worth trusting in the dark, they are not worth having any way. This filial trust is one of the loveliest traits of character.

And it is none the less lovely when brought into the

sphere of religion, and exercised towards God. If we have not a God worthy of trusting in the dark, we have not one worth keeping. If we have, then let us honor him, as did Paul and Silas, who sent up songs winged with light, and warbling toward heaven, out of stocks, and a dungeon in the dark.

As the arm grows strong only by work, as the memory increases only when made to carry weights, as the eye can see only in the light, so faith has a chance to develop only in darkness and trial. There is no room for faith in the daylight. Anybody can trust, then. Do not even the atheists so? But he who, on the darkness of the tempest-tossed waters, can trust Him who stilleth the storm, he, and he only, can claim to " walk by faith."

III.—THE END OF LIFE.

Not what we can get or enjoy, but moral culture is the true end of life.

Men ask, What have you got? what do you know? what can you do? God asks, What are you? On the answer to that question hangs our destiny. Then all things, all incidents, all gettings, all losses of this life, should be measured by their outcome, the resultant effect on our character. A possession is good, if it makes us generous, if, in the use of it, we develop all those right faculties that pertain to its handling. But if not, woe to the day on which the windfall came. Whether it shall prove to us a godsend or a curse depends entirely upon our use of it. A loss may be a good, if, through its means, we develop those graces that come from the patient endurance of life's hard and heavy things.

In either case, we are not to estimate them by what they are in themselves. This is but a superficial and, therefore, a false view to take. What they make of us is what determines their value. One of the first times I ever preached without notes, a friend said to me, "One disadvantage is, that you haven't got the sermon, now it is preached." "Yes," I said; "but I've got the practice of going without it."

A botanist makes a fine collection of leaves and flowers and grasses. When done, the fire takes it. But the best part, the drill and practice and knowledge acquired in making the collection, — these are left; and they are worth more than a dozen collections. The practice and study of collecting makes one a botanist; but one might own the collection forever, and know nothing about it.

A painter, by long years of work, becomes skilled in eye and finger and judgment and imagination. At the age of fifty he sells all his pictures to some one rich enough to buy them. He has left only eye and finger, and judgment and imagination, and the skill of all these; but these are as much superior to one of his pictures as God is to the earth he has made. He is an artist; but the man who fills his home with his paintings may be only a clown. What he becomes in his work is worth more than all he produces, or what he gets paid for it. You can buy pictures; but you cannot buy genius and skill.

Let us apply this principle to life. You have a home, husband, wife, children, property. These are partly for themselves, but in a sense quite as important they are for the sake of what their effect may be on us in our training. That is, this life is not wholly an end in itself: it has reference to a future; and one of the most important elements in its value is its power to fit us for that future. Now, in the companionship, the joys and trials of this home, you have been developing in love and patience and unselfishness and care and helpfulness. By and by the home is broken; but if you be grown thus godlike through the ministries of home, you have gained something worth more than the temporal conditions, something fitting you for the eternal home. The ear is worth more than a song, the sense of smell is worth more than a flower, the eye is worth more than a landscape, and so love is worth more than any one thing or person loved; and particularly does this appear when we reflect, that, through the loss of the objects of our love, we are being trained into fitness to have and hold them forever.

> "God gives us love; something to love
> He lends us; but when love has grown
> To ripeness, that on which it throve
> Falls off, and love is left alone."

IV.—LOST BLESSINGS NOT ALL LOST.

And then, again, the life and joy of the past were no less blessings in their time because they are now taken away. Yesterday was just as fair and bright and beautiful a day of sunshine for all of the fact that it fell off, at last, into the darkness of night.

A husband has left the household, and the home seems broken and desolate. But you are glad that he once was yours. All those years of sunny joy and blessedness were real, and none the less so that they are ceased. The loss was only God taking to himself again what was always his, and what he lent to you. When you mourn, "The Lord hath taken away," do not forget the first part of the verse, "The Lord gave;" and, above all, do not forget the close, "Blessed be the name of the Lord."

A child is taken. It made the house bright and cheery, like a gleam of sunshine. It is gone, and it is dark. But do not forget that the sunshine was a positive blessing while it remained, and that darkness is only sunshine's absence. You would not have it true that you never had and loved the child; then the life of the child, even with the loss at the end, was something to be grateful for. Add up all the sorrow, and subtract from the total gift, and there is a large remainder of clear blessing. On the whole, God's dealing has been goodness. Try and thank him, then, though with lips that tremble; and try to look up, though through eyes that are misty.

I had two brothers. They grew to be noble Christian men, then struggled with disease, lay down, and died. As their eyes closed in sleep, many a hope and plan of life faded out, many a bright outlook was darkened, many a castled scheme tumbled in ruin. But because they died am I sorry I had those brothers? Was God, on the whole, good to me, or unkind, in giving them, and then taking them away? "Good," say I, — "a thousand times good." Sorry? Nay, their memory and influence on me I count among my chiefest treasures. And then, though dead, they are mine still. I am richer by two brothers in heaven.

Will you all who have suffered, then, not say with me, "'Tis better to have loved and lost than never to have loved at all"?

V.—HOW FINISH COMES.

Not long ago, I visited the celebrated "Pebble Beach" at Pescadero, on the California coast. The long line of white surf comes up with its everlasting roar, and rattles and thunders among the stones on the shore. They are caught in the arms of the pitiless waves, and tossed and rolled, and rubbed together, and ground against the sharp-grained cliffs. Day and night forever the ceaseless attrition goes on: never any rest. And the result? Tourists from all the world flock thither to gather the round and beautiful stones. They are laid up in cabinets : they ornament the what-not and the parlor mantle.

But go yonder, around the point of the cliff that breaks off the force of the sea ; and up in that quiet cove, sheltered from the storms, and lying ever in the sun, you shall find abundance of pebbles that have never been picked over by the traveller. Why are these left all the years through unsought? For the simple reason that they have escaped all the turmoil and attrition of the waves, and the quiet and peace have left them as they found them, rough and angular, and devoid of beauty. Polish comes through trouble.

All the difference there is between what looks like a worthless stone and a gem is in the cutting and grinding. All the difference between bullion and coin stamped with the king's face is in the smelting and the minting. All the difference between a wilderness and a garden is wrought by weeding and pruning. All the difference between a block of marble and a statue is produced by the mallet and the chisel.

This principle in nature and art is no less controlling in human life. The best and truest and most sympathetic men and women are the ones who have denied themselves, and have suffered. If I wished to go to a man for help, I'd seek out one who had met loss and trial. If I wished to find a woman to employ in some work of mercy or salvation, I'd search for one who had felt the cold wrench of pain at her heart, and had learned the lesson of weeping.

God has for us up yonder, by and by, I know not what noble ministries and what exalted places of beauty and of power. Since he knows what niche we are to fill, trust him to shape us to it. Since he knows what work we are to do, trust him to drill us to the proper preparation.

VI.—BUT WHY ME?

Once more: but **why me**? Why must I suffer so much, while others escape? My neighbor walks blithely along a pleasant road where the sun shines, and the birds sing; and he seems never to be bowed beneath such weights as I carry. My way is bordered with weeping-willows; and the only song is the whippoorwill's complaint.

The answer may be, Partly it is not true, and partly it may be for a good reason that I will soon speak of. But, first, it is not so true as you think. You do not suffer so much more than others. All suffering and misfortune come not by death or the loss of property. These are even the smallest part of the burden the sad earth bears. When my brother died, I could look just a little down the street to one whose brother was not dead, who was still more afflicted than I. I would rather my brother were dead than that he should live as do the brothers of some. There are a good many things in this world harder to bear than the loss of friends. Many a secret sorrow of the heart, many a wrong, many an unknown sin, gnaws on the soul in private like a canker; and could they only be exchanged for a grave, the victims would thank God for it as a mercy. If, then, you have only to bear the memory of some noble loss, bless God with a full heart that it is not something worse; for there be things beside which these are almost gladness.

And then, if there be these differences, — which is not all denied, — I can think of one good reason which may be in the mind of God.

Not all of us are destined for the same positions, or the same ministries, or the same joys, in the life to come; and so it follows naturally that we ought not to have the same training. Here are two boys: one is to be a machinist, the other a lawyer; would you expect that the two should pass through the same preparatory training? What is essential to one would be a hinderance and a waste of time to the other. And, further, the higher the position in life for which a boy is destined, the severer the mental training, and harder the drill of preparation; so that he who has the hardest lot of study and discipline may, in the absence of any other proof, take that alone as indicating the fact that he is going higher; and so the curse becomes a blessing.

Why are you, then, called to suffer more than others? Perhaps, if you take it rightly, because he has for you some nobler work or some higher place designed.

VII.—NO LIFE INCOMPLETE.

A life is not necessarily cut off before its time, because it seems so to us. A man dies at his noon, just in the midst of strength and usefulness, just when prepared, as it seems to us, to do good and great work for the world. He is building a church; he is starting some great plan for the poor or the ignorant; he is on the eve of a great invention; he is a missionary just beginning to master his field.

Men exclaim, "O the loss!" But why? Can nobody else build churches, or help the poor, or go on missions? And has God nothing for people to do in the other life? and is he so poor a general, that he does not know where to station his own officers and men?

Martin Luther was wiser. When they tried to keep him from going to Worms by saying how necessary his life was to the cause, he said, "God can take care of his cause without me." Faithfulness in hours of duty and danger is of more value to God's cause than life.

When my brother died just on the eve of graduation, the neighbors said his college-course was lost. If this life's training is not worth any thing in heaven, they were right. But not so I view it. I take it God has work for us by and by, and that earth's drill is fitting us to do it nobly. We graduate from earth into fitness for heaven.

Light on the Cloud.

And then, when children die, people talk of a life unfinished, of buds broken off before their bloom. But how do we know that it was not the bud God wanted? We never gather a bouquet but we think the buds the finest part. A bud is just as perfect as a flower, only it is not a flower. But shall not God be permitted to have buds in his bouquet, whose fragrance is to perfume the altar in the temple above?

An acorn is just as finished as an oak. A chapel may be as nice a work of art, just as complete, as the grand magnificence of St. Peter's. A cherub is as perfect as an archangel.

What mother thinks the crowing babe, or the laughing boy of three, any less perfect or beautiful than grown-up men and women? Is there not about them, rather, a grace that is peculiarly their own? And how dark our life would be without them! And shall God have no babes, no children, in his beautiful house on high? Must all wait till they be gray, and then go tottering over the threshold of that upper home? Or shall not, rather, the glad, gleesome children, with flowing hair, and merry, laughing eyes, go smiling through the doorways to meet "their angels" who "do always behold the face of their Father in heaven"? Cannot God be as kind to them as we can, and watch them as tenderly?

VIII.—TWO SIDES OF DYING.

And then there are two sides of dying,—the earth side and the heaven side.

Here the hushed lips that shall **never speak again**, there the first burst of a song that shall never cease; here the quiet of feet that have ceased their walking, there the starting-out upon immortal pathways; here the unclasping of hands and the **tears** of farewells, there the greetings and gratulations and fresh-linked unions, and the lighting-up of recognitions that play over deathless features.

The stars that go out when the morning begins to dawn do not sink into night: they only cease to shine on us, and begin to shine on some one else; and what is to us the evening star is the herald of dawn to some other eyes.

I sometimes question whether we may not be selfish in our grief. Let us look at a case.

As often happens in our day, a family becomes divided; a part of it staying in Germany or England, and a part of it having come over here. Now, on some day appointed, an emigrant ship sets sail for America. Notice the two ends of the voyage. On the European side, the broken remnant of the household that **is left** behind **gathers on** the pier. They have shaken hands; they have kissed good-by; they have said the last words; the tears fall down, and the throat chokes up, and the heart is heavy as lead while the ship swings off, and gradually lessens to a speck on the horizon. But on the American side there is glad expectation and impatient waiting. As the vessel heaves in sight, there is a shout; and it hardly touches the wharf before the expectant ones are over the side, clasping in long-waiting arms the glad welcome of blessed re-union. What say you? Ought not those left behind to subtract from the gross amount of their sorrow something of the gladness of those who in the new country greet their arrival?

I know a family divided: half is on earth, and half in heaven. The white-sailed boat, whose oarsman none can see, pushes off for another voyage. A fair-haired boy is passenger now. Cruel and hard it seems. Could not the children stay? Why is sorrow added to sorrow? The home was shadowed before: why this additional gloom? So strange and mysterious are the ways of God. This is the earth-side view. But on the other shore the father stands waiting for the time to go by when the rest shall be gathered into the new home. And perhaps he says, "There are two: cannot she spare me one?" And while there is weeping here, there is the joy of meeting again up there. The boat shall hardly scrape its keel on the golden marge of the immortal land, when the boy shall leap out in his undying beauty into the arms of his father.

O this earth-side is only a small part of life! Let us offset the events and happenings of this by what these earthly things mean in the spiritual country.

IX.—THESE HINTS ONLY A STAFF.

And now, my friends, I have offered you my thoughts for your comfort. They will not, perhaps, take away your weakness; but they may help sustain you in it. They will not drive off all the dark; but they are glints of lights in the dark that may make your night more tolerable, or show you where to place your feet in the next steps of the journey. They only hint at the fact, that we must still take on faith, that God has always a good and loving reason in what he does. Death, a sad fact, still remains. It is still mysterious, and we see not. But the word of promise still echoes, "What thou knowest not now thou shalt know hereafter." Staying ourselves on this as on a staff, let us walk onward toward the sunrise.

MYSTERY.

O Why are darkness and thick cloud
Wrapped close forever round the throne of God?
Why is our pathway still in mystery trod?
None answers, though we call aloud.

  The seedlet of the rose,
  While still beneath the ground,
  Think you it ever knows
  The mystery profound
Of its own power of birth and bloom,
Until it springs above its tomb?

  The caterpillar crawls
  Its mean life in the dust,
  Or hangs upon the walls
  A dead aurelian crust;
Think you the larva ever knew
Its gold-winged flight before it flew?

Mystery.

When from the port of Spain
Columbus sailed away,
And down the sinking main
Moved toward the setting day,
Could any words have made him see
The new worlds that were yet to be?

The boy with laugh and play
Fills out his little plan,
Still lisping, day by day,
Of how he'll be a man;
But can you to his childish brain
Make aught of coming manhood plain?

Let heaven be just above us,
Let God be e'er so nigh,
Yet howsoe'er he love us,
And howe'er much we cry,
There is no speech that can make clear
The thing " that doth not yet appear."

'Tis not that God loves mystery.
 The things beyond us we can never know
 Until up to their lofty height we grow,
And finite grasps infinity.

1876.

THE PESCADERO PEBBLES.

WHERE slopes the beach to the setting sun,
    On the Pescadero shore,
For ever and ever the restless surf
    Rolls up with its sullen roar.

And grasping the pebbles in white hands,
    And chafing them together,
And grinding them against the cliffs
    In stormy and sunny weather,

It gives them never any rest:
    All day, all night, the pain
Of their long agony sobs on,
    Sinks, and then swells again.

And tourists come from every clime
    To search with eager care
For those whose rest has been the least;
    For such have grown most fair.

But yonder, round a point of rock,
   In a quiet, sheltered cove,
Where storm ne'er breaks, and sea ne'er comes,
   The tourists never rove.

The pebbles lie 'neath the sunny sky
   Quiet forevermore:
In dreams of everlasting peace
   They sleep upon the shore.

But ugly, and rough, and jagged still
   Are they left by the passing years;
For they miss the beat of angry storms,
   And the surf that drips in tears.

The hard turmoil of the pitiless sea
   Turns the pebble to beauteous gem.
They who escape the agony
   Miss also the diadem.

1875.

PART SECOND.

THE MINISTRY OF AFFLICTION.

I. — GOOD OUT OF EVIL.

EVERY step of human experience is a marvel; every phase of nature about us, a wonder. Beauty from ugliness, good out of evil, everywhere. The rose sucks its life from some festering death beneath the sod. The white pond-lily climbs up out of the muddy waters, and lifts its pure petals above slime and corruption. The fleece-cloud of the upper heaven is the evaporation of stagnant pools and miasmatic swamps.

And in the human sphere, the most beautiful lives are the outcome of disappointment, anguish, and tears. Then may we not say, "We glory in tribulations; knowing that tribulation worketh patience; and patience, experience; and experience, hope; and hope" frees from shame and disappointment? The roses of life, as well as of the garden, the sweet-scented flowers of character, whose savor is precious incense before God, — these, though they climb up to such a height as to overrun the jasper walls, and bloom fairest among the plants in the garden of God, do yet start from the root of some death or loss, and grow strong as they are shaken by the sharp winds of sorrow.

The old Hebrew poem tells us that it was Satan who hurled down upon Job the thick-falling storm of his troubles; but as ever falls out with malice, he was fooled for his pains. He was doing the sufferer the greatest favor of his life. For what was the end? It lifted him out of his uncertainty and weakness, and made him a strong, firm-principled man. It taught him the meaning of life. It was the means of God's revealing himself, and setting in clearer light the relations of earth and heaven. Blessed Job while sitting in ashes! How often is it that sackcloth and dust are found at the gateway of moral advancement, and even on the threshold of heaven!

II.—CHARACTER BORN OF SORROW.

The elevating and perfecting of character come largely through sorrow. This is the "mystery of the cross." All progress is by crucifixion. Experiences sad and dark, and seemingly cruel, press upon us on every hand. The past is tear-worn and furrowed, and the future glooms with shapes of trial. Like Paul, we "know not what shall befall us there." Only the Holy Spirit witnessed to him, and experience witnesses to us, that "afflictions abide in us." I murmured at this, until I saw the crosses and stakes and racks and scaffolds of all ages, and the white feet of those who made these the stairways up which they climbed to light, to truth, to Saviourhood and God. Light breaks when I see Jesus, scarred with whipping, thorn-crowned, staggering up Calvary beneath his cross, and hear those old words of the spirit, "It *became* him, for whom are all things, and by whom are all things, in bringing many sons unto glory, to make the captain of their salvation *perfect through sufferings.*" I falter sometimes when I try to say, "It is good for me that I have been afflicted." But I can now and then catch a glimpse of the truth of it, when the light of some suffering and conquering hero breaks through the blinding mist of my tears. I can sometimes see the grandeur of the truth so clearly, that, looking back over the pathway of my life, I can say, "Let every sunny spot of the past be darkened, rather than memory should lose one of the tear-hallowed places where I knelt in darkness, and prayed." Gethsemanes have deeper and grander meanings than Canas.

The richer natures are the suffering natures. Give me for a friend one who, "with strong crying and tears," has battled with trial at midnight, and in thicker darkness of soul has prayed in agony, like Ajax, for light. Shallow and loose-rooted is the tree that has known only sunshine, and never felt the wrench and shock of the gale. God, who loves us like a father, though he pities, would rather that we patiently bear our burdens than be free from them. Paul tells us, "There was given to me a thorn in the flesh. For this thing I besought the Lord thrice, that it might depart from me. And he said unto me, My grace is sufficient for thee; for my strength is made perfect in weakness."

III.—AFFLICTION MAY HELP OR HARM.

It is well to remember that the lessons of sorrow are easiest learned by the trustful and submissive. God's best gifts may turn to curses in the hands that do not receive them rightly. It is a fearful fact that we have the power of turning the best intentions toward us into the worst results. It is not the fault of the sunlight, that while the diamond gives out all its rays, and flashes a many-faced jewel, the charred wood absorbs all its beams, and becomes only a dirty bit of coal. It is not the fault of the sunlight that its beams turn one place into a garden, and of another place make only a desert. It is not the fault of the sunlight that, beneath its shining, a bed of flowers lifts up its fragrance to God, and that, beneath the same shining, a steaming pile of filth reeks offence and disease in all nostrils. These opposite results are determined by the qualities of the objects themselves. So if trouble sanctify and elevate one person, and harden and imbitter another, we should look for the explanation of the opposite results, not in the trouble, but in the hearts; for some hearts, like the charcoal, can turn the very sunlight into blackness.

IV.—TROUBLE DEVELOPS SYMPATHY.

One blessed result of sorrow, when received as a part of life's wisely ordered training, is the culture and development of human sympathy. George Eliot, who will not be accused of undue leaning toward Christian teaching, has touched the secret of this lesson where she says, "We can hardly learn humility and tenderness enough, except by suffering."

History and observation teach us that there is nothing that more frequently contracts and callouses the heart than prosperity. They who are born and cradled in luxury can have no genuine appreciation of what it means to feel the tooth of want, or the chill of neglect's cold shoulder. It is the flourishing business man, determined to be rich, who is inclined to look coldly on the suffering child, or push rudely one side the pitiful claims of those whose principal crime is being born to ignorance and want; it is the daughter of ease and wealth who can ride gayly past the comfortless tenements, crammed with filth and wretchedness, and enter with zest upon the pleasures of society or the home-circle, and be haunted by no shuddering shapes of suffering or sin: but let such as these be touched by "the finger of God," and they learn that even their petted and pampered hearts can thrill with so vulgar a thing as pain. Let them drift to the horrible verge of bankruptcy, and look over and down into the hungry abyss of want, and they learn to think of the

The Ministry of Affliction.

common pit of humanity from which they were digged. They find that community in tears marks all mankind as one. The dead hand of some friend has often introduced the smiling into the great brotherhood of sorrow, and touched the soul with tenderness for all that is sad in human life.

The thoughtless, self-contained, friend-contracted mother, whose ribbon death has taken away, leaving in its place only a tell-tale bit of crape — she now looks out upon the world through a tomb gateway, and sees all in the light of a dear white face. And, oh, how changed is the face of the earth! and what another thing it seems to live! To-day, as she whirls in her carriage through the suburb, and passes a little train of weepers, she does not hold back her pity till she finds out their station in society. Her thoughts at once go back in tears to the curtained chamber where stands a rosewood crib all empty, and to the drawer where are put away the tiny white slippers that hold the shape of a pair of little feet whose restless patter will be heard no more; and, as her eyes grow dim, all her pride and station fade away, and she is only a mother, whose heart throbs in sympathy with all who have loved and lost. And think you that in the sight of God, who regards hearts as higher than pockets or jewels, those womanly tears are not more precious than all her silks and horses and station? Not because he is a God who loves tears and sorrow, but because he does love the divine humanity that tears and sorrow indicate and develop. When sorrow has wrought sympathy, and sympathy has grown into unselfish love and action, behold! the mother has become like God; for unselfish love and action are his essential nature: therefore may the love of God permit affliction; because it is a sculptor of such wondrous art, that it can take a selfish, animal, stony heart, and by its sharp cuttings shape it into the likeness of the divinest beauty.

V.—TEARS CLEANSE THE VISION.

Affliction so washes the eyes with tears as to give clear and correct views of values and proportions.

We fix our heart on something, and soon it is taken away. This is not caprice, arbitrariness, sovereignty, God saying, "I am strong, and therefore have a right to do as I will, and compel devotion of all to me." I have no belief in such solutions of the problems of human sorrow. God has no right to any thing merely because he is strong. He has a right to do justly and mercifully, like ourselves. Therefore, though we may not always see, we must hold that what he does is love and mercy, or else he is no God. Let us look at this.

It would be right not only, but merciful and loving, for God to teach us the true end of life by any and all necessary means; would it not? This were better and kinder than to let us wake up by and by to find ourselves mistaken, and life wasted. If a ship be in peril, it is wise and right to throw any and all treasure overboard that may be needful to lighten it, and avert the danger. And a safe arrival in port becomes a justification of any measures that were necessary to tide her over the rocks, and float her on her passage.

VI.—THE TRUE END OF LIFE.

The true end of life for an immortal must be something that is itself immortal; for otherwise, when the treasure is perished, the immortal must pass on emptyhanded, and in want. To say, then, that any thing only material is the true and proper end for man to seek is as absurd as to say that the child is born to find the object of its existence in the cradle. And to see a man just stepping off the stage of life with no care for any thing but possessions and amusements, his thought and heart all untrained and undeveloped, is as pitiable as to find a strong young man, in all the vigor of fresh maturity, spending the livelong day astride of his rocking-horse.

Suppose, then, we care for nothing but wealth. If God be our father, and really love us, he would only be treating us wisely to take it away; for one of life's best lessons is to learn that money alone is poor food for the real high nature of man. We become absorbed in the pursuit of pleasure. The fair-skinned apple we grasp at turns to ashes on our lips. This only means that bitterness and disappointment must surely come to those who bend down their higher faculties, and degrade them to the level of the lower.

We chase some outward success. We miss it. Not that God does not care for the kind of life we lead; but we were forgetting the true goal. Success does not consist in bringing to pass a certain outward thing, but in the quality of character we develop, no matter in what circumstances.

Christ's whole life was a failure, judged by the conventional standards of earth. Dying at thirty-three, he stood by his cross, hated by the rabble, scorned by the mighty and learned, pitied by Pilate, deserted by the few timid ones he had taught to love him; and yet, in all the ages since, the cross has been the symbol of victory. And this outcast one reigns over a kingdom of thought and hope and love, in comparison with which the empires of Cæsar or Napoleon seem dwarfed and small. We see, at last, that the grand aim and end of humanity is the culture and development of the moral, the godlike, in us. Now light breaks. The radiance of this thought bursts through the heavy rolling masses of cloud that have darkened the world; and where was only chaos an orderly creation and a meaning appear.

VII.—LIFE A SCHOOL.

We see that life is a discipline, the world a school, and that the only way to understand it is to learn the true end of our training. The child at school, whose head is tired with knotty questions of mathematics, or who pores over some hard lesson till the letters swim and run together, and the page is spattered with tears, may think — and with apparent reason, as things look to him — that father and mother are cruel, and the teacher a set tormentor, having no better design than to ruin his happiness, and keep him away from the sunny fields and the pleasant playgrounds. But when, standing on the threshold of home, with his back on his childhood, and his face set toward the great world of earnest life, he looks out over the range and meaning of manhood, the tears he sheds are tears of gratitude, that firmly always, sternly when needful, they kept him to the hard toil of preparation. So when we stand with back turned on the then receding world, and from the threshold of eternity look out over the unmeasured range of the endless life, and catch a glimpse of what eternity means, we shall see why hard questions were given our intellects, and heavy burdens were laid upon our hearts. God forgive our weakness! we are only little children, crying over our lessons now. Then when you ask me in your complaint, "Of what use is love, when the precious objects fail so soon?" I answer, "Love is its own grand, great end. To have developed that godlike attribute in your heart is worth all the tears and heartaches of your whole life."

VIII. — A PARABLE OF GROWTH.

At the time of the first snow-fall, I heard a pear-tree in my garden sighing to itself as it shuddered in the

November wind, and saying, "To what end is summer, if it must go away so soon? Why have I basked in the blessed sunshine, and drank the evening dews, if now I am to be left by them both to the bitterness of this wintry desolation?" And it writhed and moaned in the agony of the storm. But an ancient apple-tree near by replied, "You have forgotten that you have helped beautify the garden with the luxuriance of your foliage; that you have sweetened the air with the odor of your blossoms; that you have gladdened the household by the lusciousness of your fruits; that children have played under your shade; and, more than all, that you have grown, and that you still retain the gift of the summer in full six inches of length of bough, by which amount you are nearer the sky, stronger to bear the storm, readier to meet the coming of another spring, and fitter to enter on its new career with advantage."

Then said I, "My dear ones are gone. Yes; but the influence of the summer of their lives is left upon me. My heart is larger and warmer, and more open, and I am better fitted, because of rejoicing in their light, and resting under their shadow for the coming spring of immortality, where the sun shall never go down."

IX.—AFFLICTION LIFTS UP THE LIFE.

Affliction may do for us another thing,—give us a divine discontent with present imperfection. How many a human history did David write when he said, "Before I was afflicted, I went astray; but now have I kept thy word"! The worst calamity that could befall a man is letting alone, if he be content with the partialisms of the present. From the bottom of the heart I pity them that are satisfied. There is no sadder picture in all Bunyan's wondrous gallery than that of the man whose soul was contented with the muck-rake, so that he did not care any thing about the crown and the angel just above his head. To see a man in exile is bad enough: to see him sitting down there forgetful of home and country is unspeakably worse. The most fatal condition on earth is that of the lotos-eaters, who have given up ever doing any thing, or going anywhere, and wish to be let alone to eat and sleep and dream. We respect the captive Israelites at Babylon when they hang their harps on the willows, and, refusing to sing, swear never to forget Jerusalem so long as tongue can move, or hand retain its cunning. They are men, and will yet get back to their country. But the supine slave, who is happy in the conqueror's hands, and will play to amuse his master,—him we repay with contempt or pity. The captive may be brave and generous: the contented captive is degraded. It is not because a person is ignorant we sorrow, but that he is satisfied with ignorance, and thinks he is wise.

X.—AFFLICTION TEACHES A NOBLE DISCONTENT.

One blessed fruit of affliction, then, is a noble discontent with an imperfect life, and a longing after a completer future. We all of us sometimes catch glimpses of a nobler and grander ideal than we have yet approached a realization of. How utterly short of the mark, then, and unworthy, it is to settle down for permanence in our present low conditions! A young man in college has forgotten what he is there for, and is sinking down into an animal satisfaction with the common routine of the day. He is taken up with the gymnasium, the table, the town excitements, the rounds of society. He no longer strives for honors, and is neglecting all fit preparation for the real work of life. The way to bless him truly is not to give him his fill of these things he seeks until the years crowd him out into the great world, a grown-up child, ignorant, untrained, and ready only to be the victim of strength and cunning that are stronger and shrewder than he. If you will really bless and help him, strip him of all these, though his heart ache, and his eyes weep, and put him to hard training and study, that he may come through his course a man.

So, if any of you feel yourselves "rich and increased with goods," and to "have need of nothing;" if you are contented with dinners and houses and equipages and society; if you have not risen to hunger for love and truth and righteousness, the invisible spiritual treasures of God, — then your true welfare is not to be found in getting more of what you have already. Should my prayer for your highest good be heard, it might mean the blighting of your hopes, a shadow over your pathway, the wreck of your treasure-ships, and arms empty of some friend you now clasp close to your heart. Many a man has his hands so full of rubbish, that he cannot grasp or hold the real riches that are divine and permanent. If a vessel, with all sail set, and breezes fair, be gliding over a sunny ocean toward a siren shore, where deceitful death sits smiling under a glassy sea, pray God send a tempest upon such an one, shatter the masts, tear the sails in shreds, and send her staggering over the seething billows, if only thus she may be driven off that fatal coast, and blown, gale-scarred and broken, into some port of safety.

The quaint old English poet, George Herbert, has finely taught this lesson in the following lines : —

> When God at first made man,
> Having a glass of blessings standing by,
> "Let us," said he, "pour on him all we can :
> Let the world's riches, which dispersèd lie,
> Contract into a span."
>
> So strength first made a way;
> Then beauty flowed; then wisdom, honor, pleasure:
> When almost all was out, God made a stay,
> Perceiving that, alone of all his treasure,
> Rest in the bottom lay.

> "For if I should," said he,
> "Bestow this jewel also on my creature,
> He would adore my gifts, instead of me,
> And rest in nature, not the God of nature:
> So both should losers be.
>
> "Yet let him keep the rest,
> But keep them with repining restlessness:
> Let him be rich and weary, that at least,
> If goodness lead him not, yet weariness
> May toss him to my breast."

XI.—AFFLICTION TESTS, AND GIVES ASSURANCE.

Paradoxical though it be, only that man is at rest who attains it through conflict. It was Jesus, "the man of sorrows," who said, "My peace I give unto you." This peace, born of conflict, is one, not like the deadly hush preceding the tempest, but the serene and pure-aired quiet that follows it, when the sun shines out, and the bow is seen across the dripping cloud. It is not generally the prosperous one, who has never sorrowed, who is strong and at rest. His quality has never been tried, and he knows not how he can stand even a gentle shock. The building that has stood the earthquake, and held to its strong foundations when the ground staggered, this is the one that people can run to for shelter when the coming tremor is felt. He is not the safest sailor who never saw a tempest: he will do for fair-weather service; but when the storm is rising, send him below, and place at the important post the man who has fought out a gale, who has tested his ship, who knows her hulk sound, her rigging strong, and her anchor-flukes able to grasp and hold by the ribs of the world.

When first affliction comes upon us, how every thing gives way! Our clinging, tendril hopes are snapped, and our heart lies prostrate and draggled, like a vine that the storm has torn from its trellis. But when the first shock is past, and we are able to look up, and say, "It is the Lord," faith lifts the shattered hopes once more, and binds them so fast in golden chains to the feet of God, that all the biting winds of adversity shall never break them down again. Thus the end is confidence, safety, and peace.

Such is the experience always that leads from an untried life to one proved and strong. Affliction is the crucible in which it is settled whether we be gold or not. And when once we come out purged, when we are moulded and minted, when the pressure of grief has stamped upon us the "image and superscription" of the spiritual and divine, then we are ready for the king's treasury. The discipline is over, and we are fit for the vision of God.

This glorious end it is that justifies the journey. As we stand on the hills of God, and feel the first flush and thrill of the immortal life, we may then thank our Father that tears and loss and death pursued us; for we shall see how they drove us out of animal into spirit, out of low conditions into high, out of cloud into sunshine.

I cannot close more beautifully than by asking you to stand with me by the side of the aged seer of Patmos, and, while he lifts the veil of his vision, to look with me on the outcome of earth-time struggle and sorrow, as he has pictured it in noble poetry: "After this I beheld, and, lo, a great multitude, which no man could number, of all nations and kindreds and people and tongues, stood before the throne, clothed with white robes, and palms in their hands; and cried with a loud voice, saying, Salvation to our God which sitteth upon the throne. And all the angels stood round about the throne, and fell before the throne on their faces, and worshipped God, saying, Amen. Blessing and glory and wisdom and thanksgiving and honor and power and might be unto our God for ever and ever. Amen. And one of the elders answered, saying unto me, What are these which are arrayed in white robes? and whence came they? And I said unto him, Sir, thou knowest. And he said to me, These are they which came out of great tribulation. Therefore are they before the throne of God, and serve him day and night in his temple. They shall hunger no more, neither thirst any more; and God shall wipe away all tears from their eyes."— REV. vii. 9, 17.

"HE GIVETH HIS BELOVED SLEEP."

HE resteth now.   No more his breast
   Heaves with its weary breath:
Pain sits no longer on the brow
   Where lies the calm of death.
Sunk to his rest, like tired child,
   He lies in slumber deep,
Soft folded in the arms of him
   Who "giveth his belovèd sleep."

Nay, doth he rest?   No: day nor night
   He resteth not from praise:
His spirit, winged with rapture, knows
   No more earth's weary ways.
But ever toward the Infinite
   His flight on, upward, doth he keep;
For he gives active tirelessness
   Who "giveth his belovèd sleep."

Light on the Cloud.

And while we grope our doubtful way
    Tear-blinded in the night,
He reads the meaning of our grief
    Clear writ in heavenly light.
And looking o'er the path he trod,
    Weary, ofttimes, and rough and steep,
He knows 'twas goodness led him on,
    And gave to "his belovèd, sleep."

We, heart-sore pilgrims, follow him:
    It is not for his fate we moan,
But that we "see his face no more,"
    And now must travel on alone.
He, standing on the hills of God,
    Doth brightly beckon while we weep.
We'll rest not here, but hasten on:
The night is short, the morning's dawn
    Shall greet us rising from our sleep.

PEACE.

THERE is a peace that broods in the dull air
    Above the rank green of malarious pools,
      When heaven is leaden, and the wind that cools
Sinks heavy with stagnation everywhere.

But there is death in it, and foul decay.
    The tempest then is mercy. Up the edge
      Of the dull sky roll thunder-caps. The sedge
Moans answer to the storm yet far away.

The whole earth dreads the coming, and sits still,
    Shrinking before the fury of its wrath:
      The far wheels rumble on their darkening path,
And rush to execute the tempest's will.

Through the dun clouds the lightning's flashing blade
    Cleaves red with anger; and the echo loud
      Leaps to the trembling earth from smitten cloud:
Such turmoil an unhealthy peace hath made.

Light on the Cloud.

But now the storm is over; and the tears
   Hang dripping on the eyelids of the flowers;
   And many a breach is left in earth's fair bowers;
And many a heart still trembles with its fears.

But, oh, how clear the sky, and fresh the earth!
   The tears are jewels in the bright sunshine;
   And on the trees, and every tremulous vine,
The birds to their new melody give birth.

The thrill of tempest gives awakened life;
   And all the spring lifts higher; and the air,
   Sweet as heaven's breath, and balmy everywhere,
Sheds a new peace, and sweeter, for the strife.

God holds life's tempests in his hand; and they
   Fly, swift-winged angels, to perform his will;
   And after clearing storms, the "Peace, be still,"
Spreads the blue sky where clouds have passed away

1875.

PART THIRD.

"THE DIVINE ALCHEMY."

I.—CAN HARD THINGS BE "FOR GOOD"?

WHEN Paul says to the Romans, "And we know that all things work together for good to them that love God," it is evident, that, by the "all things," he means all hard things, all rough things, all dark things. And yet he does not leave out what men call goods, wealths, prosperities: and I take it that no one who looks over the world can doubt that these latter as often work us evil as the former; that is, we are in as much need of an assurance that we shall be delivered from prosperity as we are that adversity shall not harm us.

But now we have to do with those things that thrust themselves most upon our attention,—the sad things of life. These God makes our servants. They are at work piling up for us the "weight of glory." By the divine alchemy of God's wondrous processes, though they be base metals, they are touched by his finger into gold, and made into the wrought-work and glittering beauty of the crown that shall be given unto us "in that day."

This is the hard thing for us to believe; and that it is so at first seems to me only natural. We ask ourselves, "Can such things as we see around us every day be best? Can they be consistent with a theory that makes God good? Ought we to be reconciled to them, and to trust?"

II.—IS A BROKEN HOME "FOR GOOD"?

Here, for instance, is a home. The father has built up an outside prosperity, and made a nest for the household. The mother has touched every thing into life and tasteful form within. Carpets are on the floors, pictures are on the walls, music and cheer in all the rooms. Children play on the stairs; and in the nursery the baby's crib is the throne of the family, around which circle all love and service. The mother is strong in the support of him who is the husband (the bond of the house), binding together all its activities and hopes and blessings; and the father is inspired in his outside toil by the love of the home that is the spring of his life. And it is not a selfish home, as many are, whose power is a power for evil; but it is a home like that of Bethany, that Jesus loves; for morning and evening the light of God shines down on the kneeling household, while angels hover about a spot as sacred as that where they cast their crowns before the throne in heaven.

The Divine Alchemy.

Is this an ideal home? No. I am only picturing many a home in Boston, many a home in every city and town of our land; for these houses, where the weak, troubled, fallible sons and daughters of God walk and pray their way heavenward are as dear to the heavenly Father as any fairest spot in the upper city.

To such a home as this, then, that seems a very training-school for heaven, comes death. The pillar of the household, the father, falls. It matters not under what blow — he dies. Around the open grave, the crushed mother stands with the clinging children, that only half know their loss; and their light goes out, as the clods fall, in a darkness that seems pierced by no single ray of mercy or good. They go back to the desolate house, that must be given up; and then the mother goes out to struggle with a world of which she knows little, in the brave but doubtful endeavor to keep together the children that are at once her burden and her hope.

Dare any one now say that this is good? Is it merciful? Is it kind? Is it better than that the father should live, and care for, and train and lead, the children up into noble manhood and womanhood? No! it is not good. In itself it is evil, and only evil. It is a misfortune, a curse. It is not something to be accepted willingly; nor to be accepted at all, if one could help it. The Bible never calls such things good, nor says that we ought to be willing to have them come. It is not Christian resignation to take all things indifferently, and to hold yourself in such a state of mind that you would be willing to see all loved things slip out of your hands at any time. The heart must be killed before you can come to that condition; and then you were no better than a post. God gave us our affections, and they are as sacred as the Bible, and we can never be willing to lose what we love.

True resignation is simply this: to have such a trust in God, that, for his sake, we will bear evil, and bear it patiently, believing that he will make it work out good for us in the end. Evil can never become good; but God can rule it, and make it serve us.

III. — IS LOSS OF PROPERTY "FOR GOOD"?

Take another case. A man of wealth was living in Chicago: able and upright as a man of business, he had gathered riches in full hands, until he had houses and stores and bonds. Being generous and humane, he was a helper of all good causes. Churches, missions, schools, asylums, reforms, and all the movements of our modern civilization, felt the impulse of his wealth. His home was the seat of refinement, of Christian culture, and of all humane and godlike graces.

The fire came with the sunset; and the dawn looked on his desolation. He was not simply poor. He was well, and could build up a business again; but every

Christ-like cause was weaker for his crippling, — churches were poorer, and missions were weak, and children were unfed and untaught, and every good cause was wounded, because of the calamity that had overtaken him.

Was it a good thing that he was thus crippled and overthrown? No! by no means. It was a terrible evil, something to be fought against and shunned, and accepted only on compulsion. Because God is able to change water into wine, it is no less water at the first. Because God can bring the dawn out of darkness, that does not make midnight mid-noon. Because a general can wring victory out of overthrow, that does not make the first defeat a triumph.

IV. — IS LOST HEALTH "FOR GOOD"?

One case more. A young man of marked ability loses his health in college, and thus he goes out into the world with brain-power that the body is not able to carry, like an engine in the hold of a steamer with more capacity than the old rickety hulk is able to bear. He is the depositary of learning that he can never be able to dispense: he has heart-power of love and devotion that the world will be poorer for losing.

Ought this, now, to be a matter of indifference to him? Ought he to be willing to be sick and incapable? Ought he to lie down without a struggle, and say, "It is well"? No! it is not well. It is not well either for the world or for himself. In itself it is a loss to him, and a loss to others. The only ground of submission is the faith in God that finds utterance in the words of Paul; and notice that they are not, All things *are* good, but, "All things *work* for good to them that love God." God is able to make them help us.

V.—THE PROBLEM A DARK ONE.

And now, to come close home to a minister's experiences, how often do we pray amid wrecked homes, and over dead faces! A father leaves a house that the mother left years before, and it ceases to be a home henceforth. An aged mother leaves the household of a daughter; and though she may be a ministering spirit still, she has become one of the invisible. And last and saddest of all, so far as the earth-side is concerned, a young wife fades from the sight of her husband, and, beside the larger ones, leaves a boy who shall never remember the look of a mother's face. How strange and sad a manhood must be that never recalls a mother!

Such things as these make the problem of evil and of faith in God. They are not good: they are only evil, and to be endured because we have to endure them. They do not seem consistent with the loving kindness of a sovereign God. The great difficulty is to believe in God while we look at these facts. They do not seem capable of being reconciled. Particularly is this true while the freshness of our grief is upon us. We are hardly in condition to reason: we can only weep.

VI.—GOD NO GOD, IF NOT GOOD.

But there must be some answer to this enigma, some way up out of the dark into the light of peace. Let us see if we can find a clew that will lead us thither.

What is it that Paul says? "We know that all things work together for good to them that love God."

This, certainly, is what we should expect beforehand, were it not for so many facts that look the other way. We expect to see fathers arranging all their business and plans and pleasures for the good of their children. The wonder would be to find it otherwise. And were there such a case, we should say he was an unnatural father. And were there some appearances that looked like disregard of their welfare, we should seek in his interest to explain them as being damaging suppositions against his character. And so, if a case could be made out against God of real neglect of his creatures, it would be the destruction of our faith in his holiness and his love. It is no answer to say that God is king, and has a right to dispose of us as he wills. Kingship confers no such right. Say it with all reverence, but say it firmly, God were no God, were he capable of disregarding the welfare of a sparrow, or of trampling out the rights of a single worm.

VII.—WHAT IS OUR "GOOD"

Evil can only be justified by a greater good. Not that we must always see the good before we can believe; but there must be some reason in our knowledge of God for believing that he will not do wrong, before there can be any faith in him that can walk trustingly through the darkness.

Such, then, being the presumption, let us see what we know of fact. It must all turn on the meaning of the word "good" in the language of Paul.

If health is necessary to the "good" of life, then is life a failure; for only very few enjoy any continued condition of health.

If wealth is necessary to the "good" of life, then the existence of most of us is a failure; for the rich are very few among the masses of mankind.

If freedom from affliction, bereavement, loss, be necessary to the "good" of life, the case of most of us is very much the same; for so wide is the basis of the poet's words, that almost every home is included in the sad echo of his verse:—

> "There is no flock, however watched and tended,
> But one dead lamb is there:
> There is no fireside, howsoe'er defended,
> But has one vacant chair."

It follows, then, that God is not strong and wise and good, or else that sickness and poverty and death are consistent with his being such; and they can be thus consistent only when it is true that freedom from these is not necessary to our highest welfare.

Just this is the ground of our confidence. God can take away health and property and friends in this world, and leave us the best things still. The great thing that he cares for in our life is, that we should become holy and pure and true; that we should grow up as his children into his likeness. Whatever is needful to this is needful to our "good." Whatever is not, he may take away, and not show himself any thing but fatherly and kind. Nay, more than this, he may show his kindness and love in taking them away, if, as sometimes happens, we be allowing them to stand in the way of our attaining the higher good.

The playthings, the companions, and the home, are invaluable to a child; but he who gets into a true manhood without them is better off than he who, having all these, fails of the manhood. The books and associations and tutors of college are of immense advantage to a boy; but he who gets culture and self-mastery without their aid is blest beyond him, who, with them all, comes out unfit for the contest of life. So he who gets heaven, and finds God, through the loss of all things, is rich beyond the power of language to express; while he who goes through life in health and wealth, and loving, friendly associations, and yet misses true knowledge of himself and God, is poor beyond all conceivable depths of poverty. Whether worldly goods come or go, then, is a matter of *comparative* indifference. By and by, I take it, it will make little matter with us, whether we had this sickness or not; whether we gained such a picture, or house, or horse, or farm, or office : then it will be, How did I live? and what have I become?

In the great questions of character and God and eternity, then, these difficulties find their solution. Since the great "good" of life is godlikeness, we are able to see how it may be possible for God to permit afflictions while still he loves, cares for, and watches over us.

VIII.—THE CONDITION OF THE PROMISE.

But this promise has a most important limitation. "All things work together for good." The sentence does not stop there, but goes on with the addition, "to them that love God." Why is this? Does it have its ground in God's will toward us, or in our free use of the things which he sends? I cannot believe in the former; for we must believe that God wills evil to no one, but desires that all men do right, and be blest. But all men do not do right; and all are not blessed.

If the text was an unconditional promise, we should know that, so far as this world is concerned, it was not true. We can see every day how a trial makes one man better, and another worse. A temptation strengthens one man, and becomes to another the occasion of fall. Wealth cultivates one man's generosity, and makes another sordid and mean. Power ennobles one, and makes him a helper of his fellows; and to another it is only the means of showing how contemptible and selfish a man can become. It is true, then, not alone of affliction, but of that as one of the "all things," that it works out "good" only for "them that love God."

From the view that we have just taken of what the "good" of life means, it is apparent that this must be so. If the good that these things work out is godlikeness, of course it follows that they who love God are the ones who get the good; for they who love, and they only, become like God.

IX.—WHO ARE "THEM THAT LOVE GOD"?

But what is meant by "them that love God"? Most certainly we cannot limit and narrow down this phrase so as to make it include only those who carry about in their thought a defined conception of God's personality, and who are conscious of some feeling of personal affection for him. It must be broadened so as to include all those whose sympathies and whose general line of conduct are on the side of the righteousness and truth of the universe, and who believe that these are stronger than evil. If one casts the strength of his life on the Godward side of things, then he is so much in the line of the divine movements and working that they shall help him onward and upward, instead of meeting him with opposition, and smiting him down. For God's laws help those who chime in with their tendencies and currents; and they crush those who oppose them. With this definition, then, of "them that love God," it is of necessity true, in the nature of things, that for them, and them only, "all things work together for good."

X.—LIKE CAUSES PRODUCE OPPOSITE RESULTS.

They, then, to whom affliction comes as an evil, and whose result is evil and only that, have no just cause of complaint against God. Responsible character of necessity implies the free choice of the will. This character, of likeness to God, is the highest gift that Heaven can bestow. If we will not take it, if we will not look toward and struggle toward God, these things cannot work good for us. The limitation is not because God does not want to bless all alike, but because the constitution of things is such that his blessings can be blessings only to those inclined to good. That the same cause produces opposite results on opposite things, is a truism of nature. The sun makes one spot of ground a garden, and another a desert; not because the sun is partial, but because of soil and water and seed, — differences all pertaining to the ground. The same sun lifts a rain-bringing and health-bestowing cloud from the surface of a clear lake, while, if it be impure and miasmatic, it fills the region with disease and death. The wind settles and strengthens one tree, causing it to run down and out its fibres through all the ground, clinging to stone and soil, until it defies the tempest. The same wind uproots and blights forever those trees that have no depth or grasp of root. Carbon becomes, in one set of circumstances, charcoal; in another, a diamond. The daylight brings gladness to one heart, and grief to another. A father's kindness kindles gratitude and devotion in the heart of one boy, and encourages rebellion and disobedience in another. Severity chastens one, and maddens another.

XI.—EVIL MAY "WORK FOR GOOD."

However fierce, then, the fire of trouble may be, the love of God can quench its flame. However sharp the dart that flies out against you, the love of God can turn its point. However impassable the gulf, the love of God can bridge it. The love of God turns every storm into a wind to drive our vessel homeward. Every wild beast that would desolate and devour, it harnesses to our chariot, and compels to grace our triumph. Sickness can only hasten us to that land where the cheek of health never fevers nor turns pale. Poverty is the successful operator that helps us win the true riches that thief, nor flood, nor fire, can ever seize from our grasp. Death only leads our friends and ourselves to a door that itself can never enter, and introduces us to an immortal company that never trembles at its name. There is no evil left to those who are wholly God's. "All things work together for good" to them.

XII.—APPLES GET SWEET ONLY WHEN RIPE.

But we must trust the Father for the present. "It doth not yet appear what we shall be." "Light is sown for the righteous." Mark! it does not say it has sprung up and come to harvest yet. It is sown: the song of "Harvest Home" comes by and by.

He who has never seen a wheat-field knows very little of what there is in a bag of grain; and one would hardly think that the way to develop its beauty was to cast it into the ground, and crush it under the harrow, and make it die. But wait from spring till September, and the glory of the resurrection shall display the wisdom and goodness of Him who ordained that out of death life should spring up.

So it does not seem to us the loving way of God to cast us into sorrow, to trouble us this way and that, to whelm us in waters of affliction, to bury our blooming hopes under the sod; but wait for God's processes to ripen. Fruits that are green and bitter in June are soft-cheeked and sweet in September. Wait till God's processes are finished. The turning-lathe that has the sharpest knives produces the finest work. Wait for the harvest-hour. The snows of the north are not yet gone. The winter storms have raged above the fields; but it shall appear that they only protected the buried grain, and the spring melting shall nourish

The Divine Alchemy.

the hidden life; and all the weathers of the year shall help it upward. The autumn will solve all questions, dissolve all doubts, vindicate all promises, and unfold the glory of the year. "Now no chastening for the present seemeth to be joyous, but grievous, nevertheless; afterward it yieldeth the peaceable fruit of righteousness unto them which are exercised thereby."

LIFE IN DEATH.

NEW being is from being ceased;
   No life is but by death;
Something's expiring everywhere
   To give some other breath.

There's not a flower that glads the spring
   But blooms upon the grave
Of its dead parent seed, o'er which
   Its forms of beauty wave.

The oak that, like an ancient tower,
   Stands massive on the heath,
Looks out upon a living world,
   But strikes its roots in death.

The cattle on a thousand hills
   Clip the sweet herbs that grow
Rank from the soil enriched by herds
   Sleeping long years below.

Life in Death.

To-day is but a structure built
    Upon dead yesterday;
And Progress hews her temple-stones
    From wrecks of old decay.

Then mourn not death: 'tis but a stair
    Built with divinest art,
Up which the deathless footsteps climb,
    Of loved ones who depart.

THE DEAD ACORN.

I WALKED in the field one autumn day,
   And came where an oak-tree stood
And talked with the winds of an elder day,
   And of nature's brotherhood.

I sat me down by its ancient bole,
   And mused, till, in half dream,
The real seemed fancy to my soul,
   And fancies real did seem.

I noted where an acorn lay:
   The flecked sunbeams fell through,
And the rain dripped on it day by day
   The warm, long summer through.

The leaves and dust half covered o'er
   The burst and blackened shell;
I thought, "The dead arise no more:
   They perish where they fell."

The Dead Acorn.

A gust then shook the leafy top
   Of the tree above my head,
And a shower of acorns fair did drop
   Where the brother mast lay dead.

And I heard a whisper as if they spoke, —
   Or was it the west wind's sigh? —
"O acorn child of the long-lived oak!
   'Tis pity that you should die.

"The beauty of your fair round form
   Is broken and blackened now:
No more you'll dare the joy of the storm,
   Nor swing on your sunlit bough.

"O, might one forever an acorn stay
   In the beauty of smooth, round shell,
And rock in the sunshine every day,
   The universe were well!"

While thus the soughing voice wailed by
   With a moan as of falling tears,
The dead climbed up into sunlit sky
   To a life of a hundred years.

PART FOURTH.

DEATH A BLESSING.

I.—HARD TO BELIEVE IN DEATH.

IN his letter to the Philippians Paul wrote, "To die is gain." Who of us can repeat the words of Paul? Our throats choke up as we attempt to utter them. "To die, gain? No: to live is gain. To die is a terrible necessity." So prevalent is the horrible conception of death, that it is difficult for us even to imagine how the apostle could speak so about it.

Through disappointment or crime, some men come to such a disgust or fear of life, that they rush madly over the edge of the present, and make what they call "the leap in the dark." Like the poor victim that Hood has immortalized in his "Bridge of Sighs," they will go

"Anywhere, anywhere,
Out of the world."

But this is not through any just conception of death, or desire for what is beyond. Life has become unbearable, and they fling it away.

Into this condition of impatience and disgust had Job come, when he said, "I would not live alway." He had no view of death that made him long to go, but only views of life that made him hate to stay. Therefore these words ought never to be used, as they so often are in hymns and sermons, and hours of sorrow, as expressive of Christian resignation, or desire for the life beyond.

II. — DIFFERENT THOUGHTS OF DEATH.

Different nations, at different times, have imagined death under almost every kind of figure. With the old Aryan race of India, it is the soul of the first man come to call his descendants after him to the world below, where he rules them as king. To the ancient Hebrews it was a majestic angel standing in the presence of God, and going forth with its sword, from the point of which dripped a fatal drop that was called the "bitterness of death." To the Romans it was a female figure, in dark robes, with black wings and ravenous teeth, hovering over the earth, and darting here and there for her prey. To the Norsemen it was a dark, cloudy presence, sweeping on its victims like a whirlwind, wrapping them in its sable folds, and bearing them away. The commonest conception of Death, however, is as a skeleton brandishing a dart. The skull and cross-bones are his symbols, and he is crowned the grisly "King of Terrors." He is made a bugbear, worse than those which frighten children. Perhaps Milton's picture is as frightful, false, and unchristian as any that the human mind has conceived : —

> "The shape, —
> If shape it might be called, that shape had none
> Distinguishable in member, joint, or limb,
> Or substance might be called that shadow seemed
> For each seemed either, — black it stood as night,
> Fierce as ten furies, terrible as hell,
> And shook a dreadful dart: what seemed his head
> The likeness of a kingly crown had on."

This creature waits for Satan to open the gates of hell, and then goes forth to devastate and ravage God's fair creation. This picture, from the fact that Milton stands as the great Christian theologic poet, perhaps has come to be the prevalent one among English readers; and yet the heathen Greek has the most sensible and Christian conception of death that the world has known. Sometimes in Grecian art Death and Sleep are twin boys, one black, the other white, borne slumbering in the arms of their mother, Night; and then, again, Death stands as a sad-faced winged boy, with a butterfly at his feet, holding in his hand an inverted torch. The sadness of his face is the sorrow of the mourners. The butterfly is the deathless soul burst from its chrysalis body; and the flame of the turned torch indicates the soul's descent to the under-world.

III.—DEATH IS NOTHING.

All the dreadful images of death, that are so common, are mere figments of the imagination, or the outright creations of superstition. They ought to be banished from all enlightened thought, art, and literature. They were harmless enough, just as the talk of ghosts is harmless, if only they were regarded as merely poetic and fanciful. But when regarded as real, and permitted to cow and frighten the grown-up Christianity of the nineteenth century, then the harmless fancies have become facts of so evil import that they ought to be reasoned away.

When analyzed and looked at closely, *death is nothing*. I mean precisely what those words express. So far from its having any separate existence of its own, it is simply a cessation of existence. It is not even a shadow: it is nothing at all.

All the pain and suffering and terror are but parts of the disordered life before death arrives. When it has come, it is simple sleep. It is peace, calmness, quiet. "The brain," says Oliver Wendell Holmes, "is a seventy-year clock. It is wound up at birth, the case is closed, and the key given into the hands of the angel of the resurrection." Death, then, is only the clock stopped. Or life may be compared to a music-box. It is made and wound up to play so many tunes. It runs on, now with the jingle and tinkle of mirth, now wailing a plaintive minor, now swelling with the bravery of a battle-march, or ringing with a pæan of triumph. When the tunes are all played, it simply stops. It is all there. No wheel is unbalanced, no cog is broken: it is only run down. Such is the natural and true idea of death.

IV.—DEATH NOT A CURSE.

Looked at broadly (all over the world, and through all time), it is not a punishment, it is not a curse, it is not even a calamity: it is a blessing, the wise arrangement of a loving God. Were the laws of God, physical, mental, and spiritual, only understood and obeyed, we may believe that death would generally be just this simple cessation of the run-down mechanism of the body. The diseases, sorrows, and pains that afflict life, and accompany death, — these are indeed curses, the results of sin, i.e., law-breaking; but death itself is not a curse, neither is it the result of sin.

V.—DEATH NOT THE RESULT OF SIN.

I am well aware that this last statement — death is not the result of sin — will go square against what most have been taught, and believe; they will even think I am contradicting revelation. But let us see.

The Talmud — a collection of Jewish writings and comments on the sacred books — teaches that if Adam had not sinned he would never have died, but would have gone to heaven by translation. It is the prevalent notion of Christendom, that Enoch and Elijah are specimens of what would then have been universal. Most of the Christian fathers, from Tertullian and Augustine down to Luther and Calvin, have held to this opinion. The Synod of Carthage, in A.D. 418, and the Council of Trent, in 1545, both affirmed it. All have held that physical death in the world is the result of Adam's sin. This is popularly supposed to be the Bible doctrine.

Here is one of the best specimens I know of the unsafety of trusting to a majority vote for the settlement of beliefs. This opinion has not one single particle of support outside of men's imaginations. Except by a casual reference or in some genealogical table, neither the name of Adam nor the Garden of Eden, is anywhere mentioned in the Old Testament, after leaving the third chapter of Genesis. Jesus never mentions them, or makes any allusion to this subject; and, except two places by Paul, there is no reference to it anywhere in the New Testament. From the position the doctrine has occupied in history, theology, catechism, sermon, and the popular conceptions of men, one might think the Bible full of it. But these three places, one in Genesis, and two in Paul, are all that can be found. And these, instead of being strong columns on which the doctrine of physical death in Adam may rest, give it not one particle of support. It is as baseless as any "old wives' fable" or dyspeptic dream. In all these three cases, the reference is to *moral death,* as the result of a breaking off from God; and in not one of them to physical.

And then, as a fact that should set it forever at rest, it is now known that bodily death existed on earth uncounted ages before the popular date of Adam's creation. Enough creatures had died before six thousand years ago to cover the whole round globe three miles deep with bones. Of all the dust that now is fragrant in flowers, or waves green in trees, or blooms in human cheeks, or is tossed by the winds in our streets, there is not one grain that may not have lived and breathed as either animal or man. Death, then, having existed before sin, cannot be the punishment for sin, which only came into the world ages afterward.

Pass now to some considerations that show the law of death a wise and blessed one.

VI.—DEATH THE CONDITION OF LIFE.

Dying is the necessary condition of all life and growth; and thus, if these are blessings, so is death.

"Except a corn of wheat fall into the ground and die, it abideth alone: but if it die, it bringeth forth much fruit." This is Christ's expression of the universal law, and is apparent everywhere.

The lowest form of life that is known to man is the little microscopic germ-cell, from which all kinds and grades of life are developed. This cell spends the force that is in it, and dies, contributing its life to the higher organization. And so the growth of any thing is only through the continuous death and displacement of its parts. The outer skin of the body is composed of the dead bodies of innumerable little cells that have died to form a protecting armor for the tender parts within.

All new life grows out of death. Every grave is the cradle of some new existence. The chemical elements of earth and air die, in order that the vegetable, tree, and flower may live.

The little child you hold in your arms is growing large and strong by the dying and wasting of all its parts, and the constant supply of new material; and, when seven or ten years are gone, one entire body will have died, in order that you may look upon a fairer and better, built up on its decay: why, then, should not "the outer man perish, while the inner man is renewed day by day"?

> New being is from being ceased;
> No life is but by death;
> Something's expiring everywhere,
> To give some other breath.

VII.—DEATH MERELY A CHANGE OF RESIDENCE.

Look it in the face, strip off its accidents and surroundings, and it is simply the going away of some one from one place of residence to another. The sad accompaniments, apart from the disease and suffering which result from broken law, are chiefly of our own imagining. The consciousness of pain that accompanies dissolution is generally very slight, or none at all; the languor of sleep comes gently on, the hands drop, the eyes close, and there is rest. The soul that has so many times already thrown off its old and assumed a new body, only that it has done it piecemeal, has now simply thrown it off once for all, and assumed a new one of another kind; now it has taken on not another fleshly, but a spiritual and undying one. The body left, and that we hide away in the ground, is not our friend, any more than any other of the five or eight bodies that have already been cast aside during the forty or seventy years. The new body has gone up out of our range, and left its shell behind, just as the butterfly floats off beyond the grubs that may wonder over the death and decay of the chrysalis.

One of the grandest uses of our imagination ought to be to detach our thoughts and affections from the grave and its deposit, and lift them up to the reality of our friends in heaven. By the side of every open grave, let us figure to ourselves the angel of the resurrection, and let us hear him say, "He is not here: he is risen." Death, then, is only departure.

We bear the going away of friends in this life, and, on the whole, even rejoice in it. We send our children away to school, trusting them to teachers, and are all uncertain as to whether we shall ever see them again : not unfrequently they go off for a longer stay than the one that may separate us from the last dear one who has gone to be educated and taught of God. We let our friends go to distant cities and lands on business, or to seek their fortunes ; and many a time they go away to be changed and lost more than they who die. Shall we grudge their entrance upon the everlasting inheritance of bliss as heirs of God? We place our hands in blessing on their heads, and trust our children in marriage to the keeping of other homes. We know not to what fate they go. We have not one-half the reason for trusting the husband or wife whose hand they take, that we have to trust the angel who comes to lead them up to the "house of God, eternal in the heavens."

> "O fond! O fool and blind!
>   To God I gave with tears,
> But when a man like grace would find,
>   My soul put by her fears.
> O fond! O fool and blind!
>   God guards in happier spheres :
> That man will guard where he did bind,
>   Is hope for unknown years."

VIII.—ENDLESS EARTH-LIFE A CURSE.

Whatever the first thought may be, an endless or very much prolonged life on earth were a fearful curse.

Light on the Cloud.

Picture it to yourself, of the race. At first, what frantic joy that no one was ever more to die! Friend would clasp friend, and weep their gladness in each other's arms, that never were they to be separated any more. But let the years roll on. They have tasted every pleasure that earth can afford; and they have tasted it again and again. They have visited every land, and exhausted every beauty. They have learned every truth, and discovered every fact and law that came within the range of their faculties and powers. They have drunk the cup of life to the bottom, and stand looking at its dregs. No pulse thrills with a new pleasure, beats quicker at sight of a new face, or stirs at the thought of a new achievement or a new reward. Like children shut in the nursery, they have done all they can think of, and tried every plaything, until they are tired and sick at heart. They ache to break out into some new field, or find some untried pleasure.

And then, when the world was full, and no room could be found for any new-comers (which would be in a comparatively short time), the dearest and sweetest of all human relationships must cease. No more, in all the ages, another wedded pair; never to be seen again a babe upon its mother's breast; never the prattle of children around the firesides, or their laughter on the playgrounds of the world. Homes have ceased; and the earth, full of old people tired of each other's faces and voices, tired of day and night, tired of sun and moon and stars, would wearily wait, and wait, and wait — *for nothing at all,* for no new thing could happen.

I tell you, that, as never was agonizing prayer uttered yet, these deathless ones would pray to die, — to lie down in each other's arms, and float away to untried scenes; or, if that were impossible, to sleep and never dream.

Give the race an earthly immortality, and you exclude them from any thing greater or better than the earth can afford; and they, in occupying it, would be no wiser than children would be who should agree to stay children forever, for the sake of having all the dolls and rattles and sugar-plums they wanted. No: God's grand manhood and womanhood are before us; let us go on and find them. Take away death, and we become caged eagles when we are grown, beating our wings against the cruel bars that hinder our flight to the mountains.

And then this gift conferred upon an individual, while others continued mortal, would be a heavier curse than when given to all the race. Let him retain his human affections, and what excruciating and helpless grief must it be, to stand like a rock in mid-river, while all earthly hopes and possessions and friends sweep by, and float forever out of sight! His wife would grow old; and, as she breathed her last, he would kiss her, not good-by for a while, but an everlasting farewell. The children, one by one, would grow up, and pass on out of sight. The last friend that knew his childhood would fade away, and leave him alone. How would he say, as has many an old man already, "All my friends and companions are gone: why am I left desolate, like the last leaf on the branch before winter? Let me go too, O my Father!" But no: he must make new friends; and then they would go. And so the heartrending experience of losing, over and over again, all whom he loved, would be continually repeated, until by and by the world would become to him only one vast graveyard. Turn whichever way he might, he could see only the tomb of some one he loved. And, as he looked up, he must think of those who were his companions and equals, climbing ever higher and higher the pathways of knowledge and bliss, while he was compelled to stand stunted and low in the dust, at the opening of his career. If he could cease to sorrow over the decay and loss about him, it could only be by ceasing to be a man.

An earthly immortality, then, could only be a ceaseless multiplication of earthly ills, with no hope of the compensation of those who balance earth's wants with the fulness of heaven. Death, then, is one of God's blessed gifts to his beloved. When men pray that they may not die, they know not what they ask; and God wisely and kindly treats them as a father would treat an unreasoning child. The baby cries for a knife that would endanger its existence, and is denied. We cry for a life here that would cut off all that is best and highest of our existence; and we are denied. And God be thanked for the denial!

Literature is full of conceptions of characters that somehow gain an immortality on earth. All the way down from the first, they are pictures of misfortune and misery. Old Tithon obtains from a goddess the promise that he shall never die. Aged and shrivelled and joyless, he leads a repulsive life, and longs and prays to die. At last a god blesses him with the fate of his brethren. The Witch of Cumæ forever repents the gift from Apollo of as many years as she could hold grains of dust in her hand. The Wandering Jew traverses the earth forever, bearing the unmitigated curse of a deathless life. And all the stories of successful alchemists tell how they recoiled at last with horror from the attainment of the coveted prize. No; I dare not ask God to lengthen my life a year beyond that which he has allotted me. Let my destiny be one with my earth-born brothers and sisters. If I leave not them, they will soon leave me. Let me put my hand in thine, O Father, and lead thou me as thou wilt.

IX.—DEATH THE CONDITION OF HIGHER LIFE.

I wish to urge on your attention, by itself, one thing I have already touched on along with others,—the fact that death is necessary to our advance to a higher and better life.

> Then mourn not death : 'tis but a step
> That leads to something higher ;
> There were less shining ones above,
> Did not our friends expire.

The struggles of death are only birth-throes. The life of the womb must cease before the life of the world can begin. When one is born out of earth into heaven, we have to stand on the earth-side, and cannot follow the outbursting life into its new conditions.

Let us imagine intelligence in some of the lower forms of life, and through their eyes look at a few of the analogies of dying. An old acorn has lain a long time on the ground. The sun has shone on it, and the rain has wet it. By and by it begins to swell and burst. A tiny root strikes down, and a tiny stem lifts up. It looks broken and unshapely. One day the wind rattles down a shower of new acorns from the tree. They roll about, and look at their elder brother who is dying, and speculate on his condition and prospects. "Poor old acorn," says one : "he has reached the limit of his existence. His fair, round shell is broken, and he can never repair it again. Only dust is ahead of him." And another says, "What a pity! O, if we could only stay acorns forever!" and they lament together over their common decay. But what of the lamented acorn? Has it indeed reached the end of its career? Why, it has only now begun to live! The little oakling, now born out of its shell into the air, begins to grow. It stretches itself up, and reaches out its arms, and shakes its strong limbs in sun and wind, and looks forward to its upper life of a hundred years.

Some caterpillars one day crawled around the body of one of their number, which had passed into the chrysalis state, and mourned over the change. The time had come for the butterfly to be born; but they knew nothing of this strange experience that was still before them; and so, when the grub had died up into the insect, they bewailed the broken shell, and looked sadly at the rupture out of which had gone the higher life; and they said, "O, if one might only be a caterpillar forever, and never have to die!" And, while they grieved, the rainbow-winged creature floated in the glory of the upper heaven, glittering in the sunlight, drinking in sights and sounds, and swinging on the waving grace of flowers whose very existence had been unknown before.

The higher must always come through the loss and death of the lower. Manhood can only be gained by the giving up of childhood. If the office and the lifework are ever to be reached, the nursery must be left behind. The blossom must die before there can be fruit. The corn of wheat must decay before the stalk and the full ear can come.

X.—DEATH THE WAY TO PERMANENT UNIONS.

And then death is the only possible pathway by which we can escape that which is saddest about death, — the separation of friends, — and come to a place of perfect and permanent union.

This separation, after all, is the bitterest drop in the cup of death. The unclasping of hands, the saying of farewells, the looking upon loved faces no more, these are the things that crush us. A mother goes to some old bureau-drawer, and takes out one by one, and looks over, little dresses, and unused shoes, and old playthings; and if the child is only grown up and married, or is away on a visit, or at school, she will smile over the memories of the past; and though a little homesickness be at the heart, she looks forward, and all her sorrow is lost in the gladness of the anticipated meeting. But if the little one have died, the quaint and happy memories are only material for tears; for she thinks, "I shall never hear those footfalls on the floor; the arms will never clasp my neck again; those blessed eyes will never look love into mine." The difference is all in the length and kind of the separation.

Though oceans be between husband and wife, they carry in their hearts an image of the home that will be theirs again; but if one be gone for life, the home is lost forever.

A deathless union, then, is the longing of the heart. This perfected society, cemented in the love of God, this only can permanently satisfy; and physical death is a blessing because it leads to this. No such union as that we desire is possible in this world. Husbands and wives cannot always be together: many a time the welfare of the home demands that the father work away; and it is something very rare for grown-up brothers and sisters to stay where they can, in the most limited sense, keep the old circle unbroken. Children grow up around the fireside; and just as they are getting to be companions for father and mother, one is called away into the great world's business, and another is chosen by the electing love of some strong man to be the blessed centre of another and distant home.

> "To bear, to nurse, to rear,
> To watch, and then to lose,"—

this is the lot of mothers, the fate of homes. We only sip the edge of the cup of our sweet societies, and it is withdrawn from our lips. Our hearts long for our loved ones scattered all up and down the earth, and are very hungry. But we only dream dreams that this earth never fulfils.

But, behold, here comes Death, your dreadest enemy, as you call him; and if you will only moderate your fear enough to look at him, you shall see that he bears in his hands the gift of that which you so desire, and which shall complete your happiness forever. Watch the course of those who die. One by one they pass through the cloud; and what then? They enter the open door of the Father's house on high; and as they go in, a deathless change passes upon each, and they become immortal. "No more death, neither sorrow nor crying;" "and they shall go no more out forever." Gathered here into deathless circles, no good-bys are heard again forever. Love's golden ring is unbroken, and the songs shall never cease. Through death they have passed beyond death; and now life and its fulness remain.

A little child has been out to an evening party. The lamps were bright, and the plays were long, and the music sweet, and the table inviting with confections and cakes and flowers. By and by the servant comes to take the little one home. The child cries at leaving the beautiful plays; and as the hall-door opens into the street, the chill night air blows on him, and he shrinks shivering. He clings closer to the servant, and is afraid. He thinks the transition cruel, for the street is dark and cheerless. But while cherishing these hard thoughts, suddenly the door of home is opened at the servant's ring, and discloses the home circle, father and mother and brother and sister, all seated around the fireside in the brilliantly lighted parlors; and soon, in mother's arms, all the sorrow is turned into joy.

God leads us out into the dark, but only that we may go up into his clearer light.

"There is no death: what seems so is transition.
This life of mortal breath
Is but a suburb of the life elysian,
Whose portal we call death."

GOING TO SLEEP.

AFTER the day's long playing,
    Tired as tired can be,
My baby girl comes saying,
    "Papa, will 'ou rock me?"

The busy works of daytime
    Allure her now no more;
The books and toys of playtime
    Are scattered round the floor.

Off now with shoe and stocking,
    Off with the crumpled dress:
She's ready now for rocking,
    For crooning and caress.

And slowly sinking, sinking,
    The night comes down the skies;
While drooping, opening, winking,
    Sleep settles on her eyes.

Light on the Cloud.

She does not fear the sleeping:
   Out o'er the sea of dark,
Close held in papa's keeping,
   She drifts in her frail bark.

No matter for the morrow:
   Enough that papa knows.
With smile undimmed by sorrow,
   Out in the dark she goes.

So should it be with dying:
   Drop earthly cares and fears;
In Father's arms you're lying;
   Look up with smiles, not tears.

You know not of the waking?
   Be not with fear beguiled;
For, when the morning's breaking,
   He'll not forget his child.

LIFE FROM DEATH.

HAD one ne'er seen the miracle
   Of May-time from December born,
Who would have dared the tale to tell
   That 'neath ice-ridges slept the corn?

White death lies deep upon the hills,
   And moanings through the tree-tops go;
The exulting wind, with breath that chills,
   Shouts triumph to the unresting snow.

My study window shows me where
   On hard-fought fields the summer died;
Its banners now are stripped and bare
   Of even autumn's fading pride.

Yet, on the gust that surges by,
   I read a pictured promise: soon
The storm of earth and frown of sky
   Will melt into luxuriant June.

PART FIFTH.

WILLING TO LIVE.

I.—WILLING TO DIE, OR TO LIVE?

IT has been a common and popular test of the depth and genuineness of a man's religious feeling and experience, if he were able heartily to say, "I am willing and ready to die;" but it seems to me a much better, grander, and nobler thing to say, "I am willing and ready to live."

II.—EASY TO BE WILLING TO DIE.

When we look at the condition of masses of men during the greater part of human history; when we see the political corruption, the social degradation, and the inability of the great crowd of human beings to attain any thing like the brightness and beauty and greatness of their hopes; when we see in how large a degree ordinary life measured by the standards of human ambition has been a failure; and then when, on the other hand, we see how all the eloquence, the poetry, and the art of religion have been exhausted in setting forth the unspeakable glories of the future,—it should not seem so very wonderful a thing that men could attain to the ability to say, "I am willing to die." For what, according to the popular preaching of Christendom, has dying meant? It has meant leaving a vale of tears, leaving disappointments, leaving illusions, unrealities, pains, sorrows, separations, leaving every thing that was vile, and going straight to the attainment of every thing beautiful and glorious and full of felicity. And we know that in those ages of Christianity, when the belief in the future was so vivid as to make it to the hearts that held it a grand and ever-present reality, this willingness to die was the commonest of all human experiences. Men were more than willing to die; for in the history of those ages of martyrdom and trial we see how men rushed gladly, and with songs upon their lips, to the grand privilege and honor and glory of martyrdom; for martyrdom meant simply a present heaven and the glorious companionship of God and of their Saviour Jesus Christ. And this is not a belief that is confined to Christianity either. There are millions of Buddhists to-day on the earth who have built their faith on the teachings of a man who represented life itself, in its totality, as a calamity, and who pointed out to his followers, as the highest reward of faithfulness in this life, that they should attain by and by to a state where all desire, all feeling, all hope, all fear, should be extinguished, and they should live, if they lived at all, a life that to our Occidental thought means little less than annihilation. Take the same thing as applied to the early believers in Mohammed. What did death mean to them? If they were only faithful to their short creed, "Allah is Allah, and Mohammed is his prophet," and if they were ready to join the force that had started out for the conquest of the world, rushing on the spears of their foemen meant simply the violent breaking open of the doors of paradise. It was simply rushing into the presence of infinite and endless delights. And to our old Scandinavian ancestors substantially the same thing was true. He that believed in Odin, and was ready to die in battle, leaped at once through the open, gaping wound that let out his life, into the hall of Valhalla, the Norseman's heaven; and there he enjoyed forever the presence and the feastings of his companions and of his gods. So I say that being ready to die, in the history of the past, and in the light of the religions that have been taught men, has not been so very difficult a thing, after all.

III.—WILLING TO LIVE ON CONDITION.

And the reason, I take it, that many of us to-day shrink so in the presence of death is not that we find life so pleasing, so satisfactory, not that we are perfectly contented with our condition, and willing to dwell in it forever; but because our belief in the future has grown so dim; because heaven, that was real, tangible, visible life to those who expected the momentary coming of Christ in the clouds, has faded away from us until it has become only as the remnant of last night's dream; so that we are not willing to die, perhaps, and yet in the real and vital sense of the word we are not willing to live either. Of course we should all be willing to live, and willing to live indefinitely, if only we could reach the ideal life we can picture to ourselves in our highest thought: if we could gain all the glorious hopes that have lured us on, if we had wealth, if all our friends were about us, if home was never broken up, if we were never worried until the very life seemed to be crushed out of us by the burdens we have to bear, then it would be easy, it would be gladsome and joyous to live, and we would not ask any thing better than earthly immortality. If only the first flush of the morning could last, with the dew on the grass and on the trees, and with the morning song of the birds! But the morning fades out, and we find ourselves sweltering in the midst of the heat, and crushed under the burdens of the day. If only the first beautiful illusions of youth could continue on into middle life; if we could only see all the world as fair, and believe all men and women as gentle and true and noble and heroic, as they seem to our childhood! But youth passes away, and we find ourselves battling hand-to-hand in the midst of the struggles and necessities of our later life, gradually losing faith in this man, and faith in that, and perhaps coming to the conclusion that even that which seemed to us angelic in women has about it a very earthly taint and touch of selfishness and passion like that which we find in the breasts of our fellow-men. These are the things, I say, that make it hard for us to accept the realities of our later life, and to be content and satisfied in them.

IV.—HARD THINGS OF LIFE.

I propose, then, in following out this line of thought, to bring to your minds a few of the things that make it hard for us to be reconciled to the actual conditions of our life. I shall perhaps dwell somewhat on their darker side, shading them not as they appear to my reason, but as they come to us, and make themselves seen and felt, in the midst of the struggles and difficulties of our career.

Consider, then, a few of the things that make it hard for us to be reconciled to life. You will understand, as I have said, that I am not speaking of being willing to live after the fashion we could picture and paint in our imaginations; but how many of us are willing to grapple with the problems, the facts, the sorrows and trials, just as they come to us day by day, manfully, contentedly, faithfully working out the problem, fighting through the fight unto the end, and counting life as it comes in this way a good and grand and noble thing, to be taken thankfully, to be kept and carried patiently, to be given up contentedly when called for at the end?

V.—MYSTERY MAKES IT HARD.

What, then, are some of the things? First, there are the limitations of our life, limitations of knowledge, those things that make the universe and life here on the earth seem such an overwhelming mystery to us. This does not mean any thing to children, and does not apply to them. Writing these thoughts, I am hardly writing for them. The universe is all clear to the child before he has asked any questions. He takes every thing for granted, lives in the love and light of his home, and is contented in the midst of these. But the progress of life with us is just like the progress of the sunrise. When, on some foggy morning, we look out, and can only see a few feet from the house, the world seems small and easily comprehended to us. As the fog lifts, and the light comes in, we learn, to be sure, something more than we knew before. Along with this widening of the range of that which we can see and understand, we are continually impressed with the sense that the circle of this mystery, of that which we cannot see and cannot know, is perpetually widening, until, as the fog fades off to the horizon, the horizon itself seems narrow and cramped, and we are lost in the infinity of the universe. Or as a person climbing a mountain-side: he can see, before he starts, the side of the mountain, and the little bit of landscape that is about him; but, as he climbs, the landscape broadens and widens on every hand; he sees more and more, — here a river, there a bit of ocean or a clump of trees, and away off to the edge of the sea. But along with this knowledge of his surroundings comes that other knowledge, that beyond any thing that he can see or measure there is the illimitable and the unknown.

It sometimes seems to me, and I suppose it seems so to every thoughtful mind, as though study, thinking and searching after the meaning of things, were utterly vain, so little can we discover, so little of what we do discover do we really comprehend. There is nothing anywhere about us that we can understand. I watched a little cloud of dust floating in the street one day; and I thought and felt that every single grain in that cloud had about it a touch of the infinity that makes the universe darkness, so that there was something even there that man can never fathom or comprehend. And the grandest thinkers of the world, when they have studied and thought, and learned all they could learn, have at last been compelled to say as did Newton, in those oft-quoted words, "I stand like a child on the shore of an infinite ocean, having gathered a few bright and beautiful pebbles in my hand."

The popular feeling, condensed into a phrase (for I do not think it was thought only, but the speaker felt the oppression of it), was expressed to me one day, as I was talking with a friend. "It seems to me," said he, "as though all this life was nothing. What are we here for? What does it all mean? Where will it all end? We know not where we came from; we know not what we are; we cannot define the meaning of life, even; we know not where we are going; or, at least, there is room for so much doubt or question on all of these points, that sometimes the doubts will get the better of our faith, and we seem wrapped in clouds that we can never dissipate or scatter." This mystery of life, then, comes upon us, and belittles the meaning of our lives, and takes heart and hope out of us.

VI.—UNSATISFIED LOVES.

And then there is the limitation of our affections. When I was a little child, I did as every child does: I trusted and loved everybody without a question. But do we not all know that there comes a sad and serious limitation to the boundlessness of this trusting love as we go on? Have you never felt a pang like that which came to my heart when I waked up to the discovery that even father and mother were not perfect? It was simply the necessary discovery that we must make in regard to everybody who is human; but, having worshipped and loved them, I shall never forget the pang of pain that came to me when I had to criticise those whom I had so deeply loved. And, as the younger boy at home, I almost worshipped my older brothers; and on awaking from the illusion, — for it was an illusion, though they are grand and noble as any men I know,— on awaking from the illusion that they were something heroic and grand beyond common humanity, this driving of the trusting love back upon the heart awoke such dissatisfaction with life as I shall never be able to forget.

And then we have discovered it in more intimate relations. If we have not waked up to find that those nearest and dearest to us cannot fill the perfect ideal that reaches out after the divine, we must at least be conscious that those near and dear have waked up to the consciousness that we cannot fill this ideal; and so the love becomes limited, and driven in on itself, until we become discouraged and dissatisfied with the meaning and the beauty of life.

And then there is the limitation of the possibilities of our attainments in the work of life. How little and poor and mean life seems to us sometimes when we stand at the farther end of it, and look back! What have we done? If one of us dies, we simply drop out, and are forgotten; and that is the end. What we have accomplished seems to have wrought so little change in the on-going of the world's affairs! We have been able to do so little to add to the knowledge of men, to add to their culture, to add to their enlightenment, to their improvement, to their uplifting, that all we are doing seems vain; and our arm is unnerved and drops useless at our side.

VII.—LIFE'S BURDENS.

And then there come and press upon us the ordinary, common burdens of life. I shall not speak of any thing striking or extraordinary in this respect: I simply wish to call home to your thought and feeling those things which press upon you all. We are burdened, most of us, with things that we could not throw off if we would, and that seem to make life in its ordinary manifestations to us something hard to bear. There are those who are burdened with an inherited tendency to sadness and melancholy. What does it mean? Something not their fault. The skeleton-hand of some ancestor, perhaps remote by many generations, reaches out of the distant grave, and lays this burden of melancholy on a man's soul; and he must carry it through life. If he will, he cannot throw it off. It blackens the heavens, fills the soul with doubt, puts the light out in the sky, and makes us question whether there is any God, or any love, or any order in it all.

And then there is the burden of inherited disease. Many of us wake up as we come into our earlier manhood or womanhood, and find that we are carrying a weight of which we shall never be able to rid ourselves,—a weight that makes life many times seem to us but misery, useless, valueless.

Then there is the burden of our daily business cares. How many of you at night come from the

Light on the Cloud.

business of the day, feeling that you are oppressed, worried, troubled, beyond any thing you could utter or express, by the crushing burden of your business, which you cannot throw off, and yet which it seems to you sometimes you can no longer carry! And then these mothers, burdened with the commonest cares of the household, as to what they shall do with the children, how they shall teach them, with the endless round of little petty cares that seem never to have an end, and yet that seem to wear the very life and heart and hope out of you all!

And then there is a burden that none of us have ever seen, and yet it is one that we carry, and one that perhaps crushes us more than any of these; and that is the burden of the future, — anxiety for the morrow. I take it that most of us would get through to-day very well if we were absolutely sure that to-morrow would be bright. But, however bright to-day may be, we see the cloud to-morrow; and if it is very dark to-day, the cloud to-morrow only deepens. And so we carry that which, as I have said, we have never seen, that which we have never heard, that which we have never touched, and that which we never shall see, never shall hear, never shall touch, the burden of to-morrow, crushing us down, and taking the heart and hope out of life.

VIII. — LOSSES MAKE US UNRECONCILED TO LIFE.

And then, once more, there are the losses that make us unreconciled to life, — the loss of property, the loss of station, the loss of social power or influence, the loss of the hopes of our youth, that clustered about us so brightly, that we have reached after and sought so long, and that we have so utterly failed to attain. And then there are the losses that seem harder still, — the losses of friends. I can hardly speak of these without touching you every one, for there is no home that has not some time been shadowed, there is no heart that does not cherish the memory of a face that has faded, of a voice that they shall hear no more. Many a woman from whose side has been stricken the strong arm on which she leaned feels that she cannot bear her life any longer. Life has no meaning: its heart, its hope, its impulse, have all been taken away; and she simply drags through dark day after day, wishing for the end; not only willing to die, *longing* to die, if only she could gain back the one who stood by her side, and on whom she leaned for strength, and who has faded from her arms. And how many are there, mothers and fathers, who look upon empty cradles, who listen for footsteps that they cannot hear, who see in their dreams, or in the musing hour of twilight, as they sit and think, the faces that once clustered or played about their feet, that they will never see in life again! These things come to them, and take the very meaning out of life, until death itself seems to be a blessing, and life something hard to bear; and we are ready to ask the question which Tennyson asks in the opening lines of his "Two Voices," —

> "A still small voice spake unto me, —
> 'Thou art so full of misery,
> Were it not better not to be?'"

These, then, simply as hints, — I have not intended to discuss them, for they need no discussion, but simply to bring them to your thought, — hints of those things that make it hard for us to say, "I am willing to live, right here, to-day, in my circumstances; ready to take up my burden, to carry my load, to do my work, to wait God's time."

IX. — LIFE IS WORTH LIVING.

And now I propose, as an offset to this, to consider some of the reasons why we ought to be reconciled to just this kind of life; for when we say we are willing to live, we mean willing to take life as it is, life as it practically comes to us. If we do not mean this, we do not mean any thing; for this is what life is, to the majority of men.

X. — TRUST RECONCILES TO LIFE.

First, there ought to come to sustain and strengthen and lift us up, and there must come, if we are to live life grandly, this underlying faith, — faith in the goodness, in the power, in the wisdom, that is at the heart of things, that which religion calls "God," that which we in the earnestness and simplicity of our hearts call "our Father in heaven." If, as is supposed, Paul wrote that he was content in whatsoever state he might be, it is very significant for us to notice the career through which he passed in his earthly experience, and by which he learned to be content." It is not something that comes to us at first; it is not something born with us. This contentment with the facts, the darkness, the mystery, the hardness of life, comes to us as the result of learning, if it comes at all; and it comes generally well along in life. Paul, the petted son of wealthy parents; Paul, the scholar, learned in the wisdom of his time; Paul, the orator; Paul, the leader of the faction that persecuted the early church; this Paul, himself the persecuted and the outcast, driven to think in the wilderness, and then, as he thought, compelled to take up a ministry that made him an outcast from his country, and that forbade him to have a home; Paul, who was scourged, who was beaten with rods, who was shipwrecked, who was in danger of wild beasts, in perils of robbers, in perils by his own countrymen, in perils among strangers, in perils among false brethren; Paul, travelling night and day; Paul, without father or mother, brother or sister, in his later life; Paul, without friends, except the few that he gathered about him to help him in his labor; Paul, despised and suspected in the midst of the very churches which he founded; Paul, whose life was all struggle and tempest, from first to last,—he it is who says, "I have learned, in whatsoever state I am, therewith to be content." And he learned this very much as we must learn it; for though Paul would put the definition of his faith, of his belief, and of his trust, in different words from those that we would utter to-day, yet the underlying principles on which he rested, and on which we must rest, are substantially the same. He had this of which I speak,—this grand anchor of faith in the goodness, the love, and the wisdom of God; and so must we have. To-day, perhaps, my eyes are dropping tears, my heart is heavy with the burden of grief, and thick darkness is all about me. No matter! If there be any thing in religion, if there be any God, I must believe that there is an outcome that shall justify it all. And by this faith in God I do not mean an unreasoning acceptance of a dogma: nothing of the kind. Any faith that is real and true and living bases itself in, stands upon, and must grow out of, the experience of the world; and the experience of the world has given us just such a God to trust. There is, as Matthew Arnold has expressed it, apparent all through the history of the world "a power not ourselves, that makes for righteousness." There is nothing clearer in the history of the world thus far than that there is a ruling, conquering power of right in the affairs of humanity. Those kings, those

Willing to Live.

generals, those factions, those mighty men, all those human forces that have set themselves against this invincible power of right, have been dashed in pieces as waves are driven back in an angry foam when they smite against the cliffs on the shore of the sea. Only those things have stood that have been built upon this impregnable foundation of everlasting righteousness and truth. Why, the very fact that there is any order at all in the universe is proof that there is a power that makes for order, that is supreme over all the chaotic and disturbing forces of the world. When, on some cold morning, I see the steam gathering upon the window, and see those little particles of mist shaping themselves into the beautiful crystalline forms that they always take on under those circumstances, do I not know that there is a power of order at the heart of it all, that creates these beautiful forms? When I see a rootlet in the soil, and a little stem spring up from it, and grow to a tree, gathering to itself from the earth beneath, from the air around, from the rains, and from the sunshine above, all the scattered and disorganized portions of its surroundings that go to make up the beautiful order and the growth of the tree, do I not know that in that growth and in that development is something stronger than disorganization and death? So, when I see in society, among the affairs of men, law, order, right, and truth supreme, as the years go by, ruling and regulating all the turbulent powers beneath them, coming out regnant and king at last, do I not know that the power that made and rules and works in society is a power working for order and righteousness and truth?

And so, out of the experience of the world, out of observing the affairs and facts of humanity, we may draw this one conclusion, that no argument can overthrow, and that no contrary experience or discovery can touch or weaken, this faith in the power and the love and the wisdom that guide the affairs of men. And I know that they guide the affairs of humanity, because they guide *my* affairs. Perhaps I would not express my belief in what is ordinarily called particular providences, and say that God changes his law and all his affairs for the sake of bringing about just the particular thing that I care for, that I desire; but I cannot believe in any God who rules the universe, who does not rule the particles of which the universe is composed. God does not rule all the stars in space, and neglect this particular earth on which we live, one of the stars that he rules as a part of the universe. God does not govern the affairs of this great globe on which we stand, and neglect the leaves of the trees, and the dust-particles that float as motes in the sunbeam. The same mighty and comprehensive law which holds the universe in its order is minute enough to grasp the dust-particle that floats in the air; and the totality of order could not result except for the minuteness of it. And so the providence of God, that cares for the universe as a whole, that takes it at the beginning, and holds it to the consummation that we cannot see or know, that we can only dimly guess, — this same mighty, all-grasping order of God's providence considers my affairs. Not simply nations, not simply cities, not simply families, but you and me, the leaf on the tree, the bird that sings on the bough, the flower that springs out of the sod, — these are a part of this wisdom and love and order that we call the character and the providence of God.

XI. — CONTENT WITH EACH STEP AS A STEP.

Then there is another reason for our being contented. I am not contented with what I am to-day as a finality: I am contented with it simply as a provisional thing that leads on to something better. When a man is painting a picture, and he gets simply his outline sketched, he is not contented: the picture is not done; but he is contented with the work *so far*. When a man is making a statue, and has it rudely blocked out, or only an arm or a foot, or the head finished and brought into shape, he is satisfied *so far* with what he has done, as leading to something else. I climbed Bunker Hill Monument some years ago. When I reached the fiftieth step, I had not reached the end, and was not satisfied. I was going to the top; but I was satisfied with the fiftieth step *as the fiftieth step*, as leading on to the hundredth and the two-hundredth. And so we must learn to be contented with the joys, and contented to take the sorrows of to-day, and live nobly and faithfully now, looking toward something that is to come.

XII. — SUCCESS CONSISTENT WITH LOSS.

One thought more, and this my last. We must remember, that though we gain not the grand things of life that we strive after, if we live nobly in the midst of these affairs that God has appointed as our portion, we shall have gained the grand end and aim of life. What does life mean? Success does not mean that you live in a fine house, on a fine street, and have horses prancing at your door; that you are able to command means for accomplishing whatever you wish. Success does not mean that you have attained to a certain office that you have striven after, that you have accomplished a certain work, that you have written a certain book, that you have done a certain deed. Suppose we pursue truth all our life long, and feel at the end that we have only gained the discipline that comes through the search after truth: which is worth the most, — the manhood, the character we have developed, that we have built up, or the thing that we have striven after? A man paints a beautiful picture; and the moment it is finished his house is burned, and the picture with it. The man has developed himself as an artist in the process of his labor; and this artistic faculty and power have become a part of himself, and he carries them with him forever. He may lose the outside work that is done; but the quality, the skill, those things which go to make the essence and the soul of his work, — these have become part of his own soul: he carries them with him forever. If I have devoted my life to some philanthropic labor, I may not have succeeded in accomplishing my purpose; but all that there was beautiful and glorious in that work of philanthropy I have wrought into the fibre of my own being: it has become part of myself, and I carry with me forever the result of that labor. So, if I have sought for truth, I may not have found it; but the discipline, the culture, the awakening of the brain, the devotion of the heart, the fixed resolve, the will, — these things have become a part of myself; so that, though I have not the truth, I am something better than the man who has the truth. I am the truth-seeker, the truth-lover, devoted to truth, following it to the world's end.

We have lost the toys and the plays of our childhood; but the childhood is not lost, nor was it useless. The plays, the diversions, the labors and the efforts of childhood, have been wrought into our make-up as men. So we may lose the things we strive after to-day, and life may seem meaningless to us, useless and worthless in our disappointment and sadness, when we reach after things we desire, and do not gain them; but if we are only faithful in the conditions in which we are placed, bearing patiently the burdens, taking the heartache if it comes, being faithful in the midst of the conditions where God has placed us, living nobly to ourselves and our fellow-men, we shall have built up for ourselves characters of divine finish, divine beauty, and divine glory; and these are better than to get on to-day, for this means becoming divine.

> My boyhood chased the butterfly,
>   Or, when the shower was gone,
> Sought treasures at the rainbow's end,
>   That lured me wandering on.
> I caught nor bow nor butterfly,
>   Though eagerly I ran.
> But in the chase I found myself,
>   And grew to be a man.
>
> In later years I've chased the good,
>   The beautiful and true:
> Mirage-like forms, which take not shape,
>   They flit as I pursue.
> But, while the endless chase I ran,
>   I grew in life divine:
> I missed the ideals that I sought,
>   But God himself is mine.

AT TWILIGHT TIME.

    AT twilight time,
      The musing hour,
When the past re-lives,
    And we feel the power
Of the subtle spell that awhile calls back
The treasures we've lost along life's track, —

    We sit and dream,
      Till the present falls
    In the shadow that rises
      And sinks on the walls;
And the old time only is living and true,
And dreams are the things that now we do.

    Then on the stairs
      Is the patter and fall
    Of the little feet
      That ran through the hall;
We hear the old shout of frolic and glee;
And again the lost darling is on our knee.

Light on the Cloud.

      The little shoes,
        The doll, the cart,
      The half-worn frock, —
        O! who would part
With these treasured trifles that hold the key
To the sacred chamber of memory?

      The tears may fall,
        The heart may swell;
      The loss is bitter:
        Yet who can tell
From a mother's love, what treasure vast
Could buy these waifs of a shipwrecked past?

      Our human love
        Is but a ray:
      In God's great heart
        Is full-orbed day:
If the toys of our children we cherish and bless,
Is God's love for his little ones smaller or less?

MEMORY.

O MEMORY! the cup of joy
    Thou holdest full to happy lips!
   But bitter waters Sorrow sips
From goblets she would fain destroy.

For Memory is but torture now:
    She makes the dead past live again,
    In one wild whirl of heart and brain,
While o'er the lost my head I bow.

I look through mists of tears, and see
    My blessed, bright-haired boy once more;
   I hear his footfall on the floor,
He's running through the hall for me.

I see his playthings scattered round;
    I hear his merry laugh ring out;
   I start, and listen for his shout, —
A mother's heaven was in that sound.

Light on the Cloud.

I think of all he was to me;
　　I dream of all he would have been:
　　O, had I not such glory seen,
I had escaped this agony!

O, tear the shape from out my heart,
　　And let it be I had no boy!
　　This memory of former joy
Is present sorrow's bitterest part.

And yet, and yet, — no, let me keep
　　The thought of bliss that once was mine:
　　This sacred grief my life shall twine,
And live upon the tears I weep.

Perhaps 'twill blossom out some day,
　　With flowers of hope; for heaven's sunrise
　　May follow this earth's sunset; and my eyes
May smile once more to meet its gladdening ray.

PART SIXTH.

HAPPINESS.

I.—THE PLEASANT WAY.

FROM the small number of persons at any special time in the world, who are earnestly and heartily seeking to walk in the ways of wisdom, we must conclude that there are practically very few people who believe the words of the proverb.[1] *Wisdom*, in the Bible, stands for a practical recognition of the laws of righteousness and truth, for the way of God; but the common belief of men, as represented in the prominent religions of the world, seems to be that pleasure is found almost anywhere else rather than here. The word "pleasure" is very rarely connected with doing right in this life. We say it is pleasant to do wrong; and the popular speakers and the poets have represented the flowery paths of sin, and, in contrast with those, have pictured the narrow, steep, and rugged way, the way of virtue,—a way that is rough, so that the feet bleed in trying to climb; a way that is so

---

[1] "Her ways are ways of pleasantness."

steep that one becomes quickly weary in the struggle to go higher and higher day by day; a way that is rocky, where no flowers bloom, and where they can hope for peace and rest only in some distant future. But the word of the proverb completely contradicts this supposition. It does not say that the end of wisdom is pleasantness: it says, "Her *ways* are ... pleasantness."

II.—RELIGION HAS BEEN GLOOMY.

The ordinary conception of the popular religions of the world has been one that has thrown a gloom over the present life. It has been taught that it was sinful to enjoy one's self; that, at any rate, even if there was no actual sin in the thrilling sensations of pleasure, they were yet dangerous; that we were likely to be insnared and entrapped in the pleasant things that are about us, so as to lose sight of, and cease to desire those things that are higher and better: thus the typical saint of the past is precisely the opposite of the world's conception of a happy man. The saints that are represented in the writings and pictures of the world are all men with severe faces, the men that fast, the men that deny themselves, the men that suffer, the men that withdraw from the ordinary pursuits and pleasures of life, that live in wildernesses and caves, that thrust away from them the joys and pleasures of domestic life, of society, of art, of the drama, of literature, and all the things that make up the rushing life of the composite world. These, I say, are the typical saints of the religions of the world. And I grant that this conception is a logical and correct one, if it be true that man has fallen, if it be true that the world is accursed, if it be true that humanity lies under the wrath of an angry God, if it be true that the one grand problem of life is to escape the present conditions of this world, and to attain unto something else by and by. It seems to me, then, that those men who believe in the fact of the curse and the fall, those who believe in the wrath of an angry God, those who believe in the danger of absorption in this life, and that the one thing to do is to gain a heaven hereafter, — I say, it seems to me that the men who believe this are utterly inconsistent with their creed when they teach men to be happy and enjoy themselves. It may be all right to be happy, and wear a smiling face, to take the good things of this life as they come, and rejoice in the kindness and mercy of our heavenly Father; but if a ship has sprung a leak, and the passengers are waiting for the time when they shall most assuredly go under and be overwhelmed by the waves, and if there is one possible way of escape, although it may be right to sing songs, and play on musical instruments, to dance, and enjoy one's self, yet that man is something less than human, who, in the presence of possible danger to one single human being, can relax the utmost intensity of his effort to provide for that person a place of safety, while he stops to enjoy the delicious thrill of his nerves, drink in the beautiful sights and sounds about him, and make himself comfortable and happy. So it seems to me that those men who really believe that none can be saved except in their special way, — it seems to me, I say, that these men, by as much as they love God, and hold relations of human sympathy and feeling toward their fellowmen, ought to give themselves heartily, wholly, and eternally to this one work of salvation: not that it is wrong to smile, not that it is wrong to be happy; but there is no time for smiles, no time to be happy.

III. — MAN NATURALLY SEEKS HAPPINESS.

And yet, in the face of these considerations, there are one or two facts that we must recognize; and one is, that the human heart is instinctively moved, perpetually thrust forward, in search for happiness. Whence came this instinct of search? Is it from God, or from beneath? It is, at any rate, a part of the healthy, natural life of any human soul. An instinctive, universal, undying thirst for joy is a part of humanity.

IV. — AN UNHAPPY UNIVERSE A FAILURE.

And there is another consideration. By the very conditions of the moral nature with which we are endowed, and that make us what we are, we are compelled to believe that if there is justice, if there is righteousness, if there is love, on the throne of the universe, the grand end and outcome of the universe must be one of joy, of happiness, of peace. I hesitate not to say, and I believe that the sense of justice of the world will by and by echo the saying, that if it should be that one, the least and most despised human being, was to remain in some outcast corner of the universe, sad, burdened, stricken, woeful, wailing, forever, then the sum total of the joy and the songs of heaven, all the thrilling pæans of triumph of those who have fought and come off victors, all the ten million times ten million of joyful souls in heaven, would not take away from the fact that the universe, as a whole, was a failure, a discredit to its original, a disgrace forever blotching the throne of the Almighty. For we must feel that, however essential it be that the world be right, — and it must be right because right is the way to God, to blessedness, and to peace, — yet, if making the whole universe right made us all miserable, our very conception of morals would have to be reversed; for we cannot possibly conceive that the outcome of righteousness, of truth, of divine thinking and divine living, can be any thing else than what we are compelled to conceive as divine blessedness and divine joy.

V.—PLEASURE IS LIFE, AND PAIN IS DEATH.

There are several considerations that go to support and strengthen this statement of ours, that happiness is rightfully an object of human search. It is based in the physical facts of our nature. It is now distinctly ascertained as a scientific fact, — perhaps few have ever thought of it in that way, not having had it presented to them; but it is distinctly ascertained to be a fact of man's bodily, mental, and spiritual life, — that those sensations which give us pleasure really do add to the sum-total of life; that every painful or disagreeable sensation takes something away from the fund of man's power and the duration of his being. So that the old proverb was wiser than we were perhaps aware, when it declared that "every sigh drives a nail into a man's coffin, and every laugh draws one out." It is not simply that men are happier, that they rejoice more, that they look and feel well; but as a physical fact, touching health and touching life, it is true. You have experienced it a thousand times, perhaps, without stopping to interpret it. You get up some morning, and perhaps it is cloudy; the day is disagreeable; you feel the effects of your surroundings: and so your own sky is cloudy, and your disposition is full of the east wind. Every thing goes wrong with you, as you say, on such a day as that. It is hard for you to do any thing. You feel depressed. Your heart is heavy;

your pulse beats slowly and without any force; you are tired and weary. It is on such a morning as this, if you be a husband, that the wife is glad when breakfast is over, and you are gone to business. It is a morning when the cat and the dog, if they are wise, keep out of your way, — a morning when every thing is disagreeable and hard to you. But perhaps, in the midst of all this, there comes in some friend, and his talk is cheery; he tells some anecdote that starts the pulsations of life; or you hear a piece of good news, — some project in which you were intensely interested has succeeded; something has happened to start in you a pulsation and thrill of joy: and there is really an addition, instantly, to the sum-total of your physical life. The eye brightens, the face flushes, the pulse is stronger and more rapid, the heart throbs with a more manful beat, and the whole man is lifted up to a higher plane. You can think better; you can do more; you are more of a man in every way; and it is simply the pleasurable sensation that has created this difference, and changed your apparent oppression into strength and vigor.

Perhaps you remember that simple story (I tell it because it is so simple, and because it so aptly illustrates my point) of the professor who took some small children out into the woods for an afternoon frolic and study; and when they were two or three miles from home, he found that some of the smaller ones especially had grown so weary that it was really a serious problem with him as to whether he would be able to get them home. At last the childish device occurred to him, of sending them off into the woods to cut branches of willow, that they might ride them, child-fashion, as their horses, toward home. The idea struck their childish fancy; a sense of joy came over them; they were playing then, working no longer; and having mounted their horses, without one thought of weariness or care, they found themselves speedily at their own doorways again. Now, this was not fancy. This change from sadness, from depression, from physical weakness and inability, to strength and joyous activity, was simply a change from a painful sensation to a pleasurable one. It indicates a power which we find in every human heart, in every human body and soul.

VI.— HAPPINESS ESSENTIAL TO BEST WORK.

And then it is a fact that is testified to by the experience and observation of mankind, that the best work of the world is done by those who are happy in their work; that is, happiness is an element of all successful work. If you attempt to do something that is disagreeable to you, that you do not like, not only is it hard to do, but you are certain not to do it well. We speak sometimes of the necessity of a man's "following the bent of his genius" if he would be successful. What does that mean? It means simply this: that it is a physiological fact, a fact of human nature, we are so constituted that the exercise of any healthful faculty is a pleasure to us. We are capable of doing a hundred different things, perhaps; and if we are capable of doing every one of those hundred things with equal pleasure, that is, if we are just as much drawn to this one as to that, or to one as to the other, then there is no bent to our nature; there is no special reason why we should follow one pursuit more than another. But most of us are so constituted that we lean over, we bend, in some certain direction; that is, the faculties of our being reach out more forcibly, more strongly, in some one direction than they do in another. So one man wants to be a banker, another a lawyer, another a minister, another a farmer, another a mechanic, another a musician, another an artist; that is, the preponderance of their faculties bends in one way or another. And it is the men who follow their bent, who do the things they like, — who, in other words, pursue pleasure in their work, — these are the men who have done the finest and grandest work of the world. Shakspere could not have succeeded so well in any thing else but as a poet and dramatist. Compel Milton to have turned artist, and he would have been a third or fourth rate one. So take an artist, and attempt to make a poet of him, and you will fail. Each one follows the bent of his faculties, which is in the line of his happiness and joy.

VII.—THIS THE ROOT OF CIVILIZATION.

Then there is another truth, wider and broader even than this, if it be possible. It is this thirst for pleasure, this thirst for gratification, which is the very root of the world's civilization. I care not what it is, — from the clearing of the forest in primitive times or away out on the frontiers, to the putting in their places, in the Exposition at Philadelphia to-day, of the finest and highest results of human activity: the principle I have laid down will hold true everywhere, that this thirst for pleasure, this desire for happiness, is the root of the world's achievements and civilization. Why does a man go out into the wilderness, cut down trees, break up the soil, start a new settlement, and build around him a home? What is it that is the mainspring of this activity? What is the power that levels trees, that digs up their roots from the soil? What is it that breaks the ground, plants the seed, lays out the garden-plat, builds the home, and beautifies it all within? It is simply the desire to satisfy the social nature of man: it is love, and seeking for the gratification of love. This one principle has been the mainspring and the motive force of it all.

And so in society, in government, what is the mainspring of the governmental life of the world? It is simply the earnest desire of man to search for happiness, that arranges the broadest and deepest foundations and conditions for the stability and permanence of that happiness. You remember the opening words of the immortal Declaration, that comes to us so vividly in our centennial year. What did Jefferson say was man's inalienable right? "The right to life, liberty, and "—this is the culmination, this the thing for which life and liberty themselves are desirable—"*the pursuit of happiness.*" This is the end and object of it all,—the end for which governments are established; for justice itself, and even our police regulations, and all the darker and more horrible sides of government, such as is often illustrated by the hanging of some poor wretch,—all these things, have their root in this desire for happiness; for society, even at the cost of quenching the life and peace and joy of one individual, seeks the happiness of those defenceless ones who else would be destroyed. So the principle is the same, and runs through it all.

VIII.—OUR RIGHT TO HAPPINESS LIMITED.

But there are one or two limitations to the rightfulness of this search after happiness, on the part of mankind; and the most important of them all grows out of the fact that we live in society. If I alone existed in the State of Massachusetts, then I would have a perfect right to be grasping and greedy; to take into my arms, if I could, every thing in the way of the resources and powers and opportunities and pleasures that that State could afford. But I am not alone. If there were only two of us, then I might take one-half that the State afforded. But the State is thronged with a busy population. Therefore this right of search for happiness is limited by this one principle. You and I may search for it anywhere, everywhere, by any lawful means, so long as we do not trench upon the right to search for happiness of some other human being. "Human," did I say? I will broaden it. I will not confine it to humanity. I believe that on the part of the civilized world, as yet, there is only partially developed the respect that we ought to have for the rights of other sentient life. You have no right, for the sake of pleasure, to trench upon the life and happiness of your horse, your dog, or your cat. You have no right to trench on the life and happiness of the birds in the trees, or the wild beasts in the forest; and I think somewhat less of that man than I otherwise should, who is capable of enjoying what is called "sportsmanship" at the expense of the life and pleasure of others, and with no higher object in it than simply his personal enjoyment. I believe Cowper gave utterance to a grand truth, which will some time be recognized as a universal principle of morality, when he said, —

"I would not enter on my list of friends
 (Though graced with polished manners and fine sense,
 Yet wanting sensibility) the man
 Who needlessly sets foot upon a worm."

The worm has rights, according to the measure of its

life and ability, the same as you. You have a right to quench those rights at the bidding of some higher principle or truth, but not at the bidding of your own caprice, or for the sake of your own passing pleasure.

I say, then, that this principle finds its limitation chiefly in the relations that we sustain to our fellow-men and to all our fellow-beings. And here comes in the one principle that ought to guide us in our social life. Take one of the commoner and darker phases of the violation of this principle, — one that I need hardly speak out, and yet would not pass by. What has become of the principle, of the manhood, of the honor, of the virtue, of the truth, of the sensibility of that man, who, for the sake of his own passing pleasure, trenches upon the rights of another home, or who is willing to take pleasure at the price of the reputation, the standing, the life, of some other human being, — leaving, perhaps, some one who might have been a noble woman, and the centre of a noble home, stranded, outcast, scarred, and broken, cast over the side of the pathway along which human progress travels? If you will but think of it, and analyze the principle that makes a man capable of enjoying himself at the cost of others in such a way as this, you will see that if it only be carried deep enough, and filled full enough with passion, and made strong enough, it is simply a realization of our deepest and most terrible conceptions of that which is most darkly satanic. Devilhood itself means nothing more than this: a seeking for pleasure, a seeking to carry out the individual will of the person, for his own gratification, without any regard to the price that must be paid by the victim of his desires.

IX.—HEALTH A CONDITION OF HAPPINESS.

I pass now, after touching upon these principles thus, to consider two or three conditions of human happiness. How shall we seek to be happy? The first and most common condition, the one that lies at the foundation of all, is expressed in the one word *health*. I do not mean simply physical health: I mean health of body, health of mind, health of soul; that is, right relationship between the different parts of our own being, and between our own being and our physical and social surroundings. You can remember a time, if you have become too wearied and diseased with the cares and burdens of life to feel it to-day, and you know some one who stands for a representative of it to-day, to whom simple existence is ecstasy. Opening the eyes, and letting the light come in, is joy. Simply stretching the muscles, and feeling the power of the arm, gives a thrill of pleasure. To feel the air fan the cheek is a delight. The consciousness of physical vigor is a constant joy; and, where health is, it will always be so. When a man feels the touch of the east wind as a pang of pain, he may know that the time of his perfect health has passed by. If the eye is diseased, the falling of the gentle, beautiful light of

Happiness.

heaven upon it is a pang of pain. And so I say of any faculty, whether physical, mental, or spiritual: the simple use of it carries with it a sensation of delight if there be health in that faculty; so that the one grand condition that lies at the foundation of all the pleasure of life is represented by this one word *health*.

You take an instrument to-day, string it in perfect accord, and place it in the window where the breeze will play over its strings; and, if it is attuned to the wind, there will come on the air a dreamy sound of lulling music. And so this human nature of ours, this physical, mental, and moral life, if it be attuned perfectly to the forces of the world about us, every breath of the world's life over us will be music; so that we need not go far to search for joy. Simply opening your eyes, simply reaching out your hand, simply moving your foot, will be, of itself, happiness.

But, through our ignorance or carelessness, the most of us have altogether too little practical control over the matter of health, — though it is to our shame that, by reason of our ignorance and lack of self-control, we are not able to command the question as to whether we shall be well or not. (The world will some time come to it, when it will be able to be well at will.)

X. — APPRECIATION OF COMMON THINGS.

But another condition, more within the reach of all of us at present, and perhaps more important even than the one to which I have referred, is the appreciation of the common things of the world. The most of us have within our reach abundant means for constant joy and happiness; and the reason we are not happy is because, overlooking these, we are reaching for something that we have not, and crying after that. You remember the story of Haman and Mordecai, in the book of Esther: how Haman, the first one in all the kingdom, had every human being save the king himself at his feet, except one Jew, who sat stiff-necked at the king's gate, and would not bow to him as he went by. He thought about that so exclusively and continually that it entered as a bitter drop into the cup of his pleasure, and vitiated every joy. "Of what avail," he said, "is it to me that I am the first man in the kingdom, that every man bows to me, that my word is law to the farthest extreme of the empire,— what good is all this to me so long as Mordecai sits there, and will not bow as I pass by in the street?" That is an illustration of the readiness with which many men throw away abundant sources of pleasure just because their will, that they like to make so universally regal, is balked in some little particular. We are as wise and no wiser than the little babe in her mother's arms, who throws away her doll, throws away her rattle, throws away all her playthings that strew and litter the floor, and, from the window, cries for the moon.

If you will but think of it, the most precious things

Happiness.

are the commonest things. The very best gifts that it is possible for God to bestow upon humanity, he has already bestowed upon every man, woman, and child in the world. The most priceless gifts are common things that everybody has, — light, air, physical existence, mental and moral powers and capabilities, the gratification of love, the power to build a home, to have a wife by your side, and children about your feet. The common things of the world, — how priceless they are! Iron is worth a thousand, a million, times more than gold. You might take gold out of the civilization of the present time, and that civilization would hardly be touched; but if you took iron out, you would make civilization itself an impossibility. Iron, that we tread on in the streets, and think nothing of, is the minister to all our pleasures; and yet men, for envy of a jewel, a gewgaw, a ring, a gem of some kind, simply for adornment, will throw away the vast fund of pleasure that comes to them from God's universal gifts, trampling them under their feet as swine tread pearls in the mire, and then question the wisdom and the love and the bounty of God, because he has not given them something which is really worth to them very little, after all.

If you will only look over this world in the light of this principle, you will find it true, I think, that God is more equable in the distribution of his gifts than you imagine. The man who has the largest pile of wealth is able only to get out of it his board and clothes.

He may board in a finer house, and have a little better quality of clothes; but it is an infinitesimal part of the largest fortune that any man can use. So he who has what he can use is just as rich as the man who has so much that he is burdened everlastingly with the care of it.

I do not wish to press this principle too far, only to emphasize again this one idea that the central things, the most precious things, those things on which human happiness depend, are universal things. Take it at your dinner, say: what are the things which you could best spare, and what are the things that you would think no dinner could be complete without? They are the things which you give to the prisoner as his prison fare. They are the very centre and foundation of your physical life, the things that no man can do without,—bread and water, the two universal elements of life. You can spare all the side-dishes; you can spare every thing else: you cannot spare these; and the poorest, if he have any thing, has these.

XI.—NOBLE HAPPINESS IN NOBLE THINGS.

If you wish to gain a happiness that is permanent, a happiness that will grow as your being grows, you must constantly seek to cultivate the higher and nobler side of your being. Cultivate those things that are permanent; build yourself up in those things that are divine. Bodily pleasures are transient in their very nature. Take any one of the nerves of the body, and confine the sensations of pleasure to that one nerve, that is, play on that one string day after day, and in a very little time the sensation of pleasure turns to a sensation of pain, and pain becomes disease, and disease destruction of the very source of pleasure. If you take a violin, and play for a month on one string, you not only do not make fine music, but you wear that string out, so that there is no music left in it at all; thus if you play on any one string of this marvellously attuned instrument of the body, of the mind, and of the soul, that makes up the man, you will find that you are destroying the very capability of pleasure. This is what the sensual man does; this is what the man does who makes the pursuit of money the only thing in life out of which he can get any pleasure; this is what the man does who makes himself a bookworm, and buries himself in his books, or who makes ambition the one object of his life. In other words, a man should have more than one string to his instrument, and should play various tunes, if he would have melody and harmony in his life.

Enjoy to the full the sweets of this present life that God has given you. There is no harm in it: there is good in it, if you keep inside the laws of right, the laws that govern your relations to your fellow-men. Train yourselves mentally, because you are capable of thought. Did it ever occur to you that the word *man* is derived from a root that means *to think?* Man is a thinker; and no being has any right to call himself a man, who does not cultivate his power of thought, broaden himself out, search for truth, look for the higher and nobler things of life.

XII.—THE NOBLE THINGS ENDURE.

Then the permanent things of life, that fill up the measure of our satisfaction, and reach out into the future, are those that link us to the qualities that are indeed divine. Love, goodness, truth, righteousness — these are the springs of inexhaustible joy. And the obligation comes in just here. *May*, translated, becomes *ought;* that is, a man *ought* to be all he can. If a horse is capable of grand speed, of doing the highest and finest work that is possible to the horse, if that horse could be consciously contented with doing something less, something poorer, dragging a cart, and simply working in the drudgery of the world, he would have fallen below that which he was capable of, and might be morally condemned as having become less than he was strong enough to become; but what shall we say of a man who, being crowned with the possibilities of an intellectual and spiritual life that link him with the highest beings of the universe, and with God, is contented to live on the plane of the animal; living entirely here, finding his satisfactions here, caring for nothing grander and better? He not only comes under condemnation as having done wrong, but he loses higher, broader, grander sources of joy; because, as you go up to God, you are not climbing a pyramid, broad and grand at the base, but coming to a point at the top: you are following one single ray of light until it broadens and widens, and the whole heaven is aglow, and you come to the very source of light itself. So as you travel from humanity toward God, toward heaven, your pathway broadens and brightens, just according to those beautiful words of the Bible: "The path of the just is as the shining light that shineth more and more unto the perfect day."

GOD MADE OUR LIVES TO BE A SONG.

GOD made our lives to be a song
    Sweet as the music of the spheres
That still their harmonies prolong
    For him who rightly hears.

The heavens and the earth do play
    Upon us, if we be in tune:
Winter shouts hoarse his roundelay,
    And tender sweet pipes June.

But oftentimes the songs are pain,
    And discord mars our harmonies:
Our strings are snapped by selfish strain,
    And harsh hands break our keys.

But God *meant* music; and we may,
    If we will keep our lives in tune,
Hear the whole year sing roundelay,
    December answering June.

God made our Lives to be a Song.

> God ever at his keyboard plays,
> Harmonics, right, and discords, wrong;
> "He that hath ears," and who obeys,
> May hear the mystic song.

HOPE.

HERE, standing by the sleeper's side,
    Pale face, closed eyes, and restful feet,
    Cold hands in nerveless clasp that meet,
Can I think aught but that, *He died?*

And when the grassy mound is piled,
    Must I bend o'er the flowers above,.
    And say, " The one I loved and love,
My husband, father, brother, child, —

"The hands I held, the lips I kissed,
    These are but dust and ashes now,
    Changing to shrub or flower, and know
The *friend* will be forever missed"?

Nay, let the dust go back to dust:
    Nature will have her own; but yet
    The *body* payeth Nature's debt;
And room is left for grandest trust.

Hope.

As, in the sacred memory
   Of days of old, the angel stood
   Beside the orphaned brotherhood,
And startled them with his strange cry, —

"He is not here: he's risen!" so now
   Hope stands, bright-winged, above the sod,
   Pointing up to the house of God, —
Bidding us not to look below.

Not in the past, not in the ground,
   Do those we call the lost abide:
   Some day we'll see them at our side,
The lost no more, but then *the found*.

Thus whispers Hope; and we believe
   Her whisper is an echo sent
   From God o'er heaven's bright battlement:
And that God never would deceive.

PART SEVENTH.

HEAVEN.

I. — WHERE IS HEAVEN?

NOT as a mere matter of curiosity do I propose to lead you along the pathway of human speculation on this question. Perhaps it were worth while to do it even for no higher purpose. But as to the man, the thoughts of his childhood, and the line of his growth, are instructive and encouraging, so, to the Christian manhood of the world, its childish thoughts, and methods of youthful progress, are full of meaning, and of food for hope.

The belief of mankind, that a soul survives the body, may be regarded as an inherent and universal instinct; for there is no well-founded account of an exception to this belief anywhere on record. Some of the rudest barbarous tribes seem to have attained no conception of any special abode for these souls, but imagined that they staid around the places of their old residence, or of their burial. The next step beyond this perhaps may find illustration in the beliefs of our

North American Indians. Their imaginations took different forms in different tribes. I give one as a sample. They "believe that beyond the most distant mountains of their country there is a wide river; beyond that river, a great country; on the other side of that country, a world of water; in that water are a thousand islands, full of trees and streams of water, and that a thousand buffaloes and ten thousand deer graze on the hills, or ruminate in the valleys;"[1] and he thinks, —

> "Admitted to that equal sky,
> His faithful dog shall bear him company."

And Hiawatha, leaving his people for "the land of the hereafter," sails in his birch canoe westward over the northern lake, following the purple track of the setting sun, and disappearing in the golden mists of the distance.

About on a level with this were the early Grecian and Oriental dreams. The garden of the Hesperides, with its dragon-guarded golden apples, in the far West; the celestial cities of Meru, with towers that touched the sky; the banquet-halls of Ethiopia, mirage-like in the desert; the spicy Islands of Immortality, musical and enchanting in mid-ocean; the happy country of the Hyperboreans, nestling amid the summits of Northern Caucasus, — these are some of their fancies. Others were of Elysian Fields in Hades, or of

[1] Dick's "Future State," p. 20.

Islands of the Blest, away somewhere near the borders of the world.

These may suffice for hints of Old World thoughts and hopes. We must now confine ourselves to the line of Hebrew and Christian speculation.

Wherever the Scriptures were known, the cherished traditions of the Garden of Eden were preserved. And as the evil of the world all centred in the loss of that, so naturally, hopes of recovery would take on the form of getting back to Eden once more. Therefore speculation strove to settle the location of the Garden, and to fix there man's hopes of the future. Sometimes it was located deep in the recesses of India; again, in the beautiful valleys of Georgia, rose-decked and spice-perfumed; and then in some unexplored region of Mesopotamia. The fainting traveller in the desert would imagine he caught glimpses of its playing fountains and waving palms. Or, it was in the centre of the torrid zone; the hot flaming, fiery sword guarding it, on every hand, against mortal approach. In a Latin work of the twelfth century, it is said, "Paradise is the extreme eastern part of Asia, and is made inaccessible by a wall of fire surrounding it, and rising unto heaven." Since then the Canaries have been thought to be Elysian, and so were named "The Fortunate Isles." And among the motives that animated Columbus in his voyages, no small place should be assigned to his hope of finding the seat of the primeval paradise; and all readers of history know with what intense eagerness the Spanish explorers searched the mysterious depths of this Western world, in hopes of somewhere coming upon the long-sought terrestrial paradise ; and the old Spanish hidalgo hoped to cast off his years again when, somewhere in Florida, he should discover and bathe in the fountain of perpetual youth.

But, as geography has advanced, these mirages have fled ; and as the common light of day shone in, the dreams have dissolved and faded. Not on the surface of the earth is it to be found.

The ancient Jews conceived of Sheol as beneath the earth ; and, in early Christian times, they located paradise in one part of this underground world. Even Dante, so late as the year 1300, teaches a similar doctrine. Science has made it forever impossible that these opinions should prevail again.

A widespread belief of Christendom has been, that this world, purged and renovated by fire, is to be the future heaven of the race. There are some pleasant things about this conception, that commend it at first to the popular mind. But almost its only basis is certain passages of Scripture about "new heavens and new earth ; " and as these doubtless refer to moral and spiritual renovation, rather than physical, their support fails. It necessitates material bodies also in the future life, or rather presupposes them ; and, further, since there is no proof, but much the other way, in favor of this world's coming to an end, for untold ages yet, it appears extremely improbable that Seth and Abraham and Moses and Paul have yet to wait for millions of years before they can get their bodies, and enter their final rest.

I can only touch briefly on other forms of belief, before coming to the one I am most inclined to adopt. Some have placed heaven in the moon. Books have been written to prove it in the sun. Others locate it on Alcyone, the central sun of our firmament, the milky way; and by a still grander flight of imagination, and with more of reason, if it is to have any one great orb to itself, still others fix it in the grand central sun of the universe, around which revolve and shine all other suns and systems, galaxies and firmaments. That there is such a central light, science seems to indicate, and men are coming to believe; and, were I to choose among the various material locations that have been fixed upon, I should unhesitatingly select this as the grandest and most reasonable. But there is one other theory, grander and more worthy still.

It will be apparent to you by this time, from the various and conflicting beliefs of Christendom, that the Bible does not answer the question as to the location of heaven. But as, when your friend goes to Europe, you cannot help giving the place to which he has gone some kind of picture and outline in your mind, so the history of human thinking proves that men must and will give some "local habitation" to their future hopes. And the best we can do is this: by the light of Scripture, of science, and our own natures, we may think the noblest and most reasonable thing we can; and we may be sure that, whether our notion is right or wrong, the reality will not disappoint us. We cannot fancy any thing that will equal the fact; and so I do not here offer my dictum as necessarily true: I only give it as the best I can now think. If any of you can think a better, keep it. All our mistakes will be corrected by and by.

II.—MOST REASONABLE THOUGHT OF HEAVEN.

What, then, is the situation? It was natural enough that the ancients should locate heaven as they did, having their extremely limited knowledge of the universe. They thought this earth was all, and its duration brief: so they had only to provide for its comparatively few inhabitants. Now, we know that this world is only one little grain of sand on a limitless beach of worlds, on which the ocean of infinity breaks. As for its duration, there is not the least particle of reason for supposing that the universe, in some form or other, shall ever cease to be; and the number of God's children for whom a heavenly place is prepared, who shall count them? Not only the innumerable millions of earth. There is every reason to suppose that the number of inhabited worlds is as great as the number of sand-grains of this; and these shall cease being the birthplaces, cradles, and training-schools of intelligent creatures, who can tell when? In the light of these considerations, it seems to me extremely unreasonable to suppose that all these are to be confined, for a home, to any one orb of however magnificent proportions. God may make some peculiar manifestations of himself at the centre, and so it may be the temple of the universe.

There are animals in existence as much smaller than man as he is smaller than the whole universe; and the ultimate particles that compose the human frame are as far apart, according to their size, as the suns and stars of the astronomic system; and the universe may look to God as much like one compact and connected mechanism as does a brick or brownstone dwelling to us. I incline to adopt the belief, then, that the universe is God's "house," and that the worlds and interstellar spaces are its "many mansions," or rooms. It seems to me the most magnificent conception of immortality that I have ever met. I will only attempt to indicate one or two points in its support. Nothing in the Bible or in reason, that I know of, necessitates its rejection.

III.—THIS IDEA GIVES ROOM.

It gives room and range as no other theory does. Science cannot outgrow it, as it has so many others. It makes place for the countless children of God on countless other worlds.

IV.—ANALOGY SUPPORTS IT.

A strong argument may be drawn from analogy. The whole world is packed full of life. A drop of water is a little world in itself: it is all alive with thousands of creatures. Every summer leaf is thickly inhabited. Not a point on the globe, large enough to place the end of your finger, but may be all crowded and moving with creatures as wondrous in structure as man. It is contrary to what we know of God's ways, then, to suppose immense abysses empty between all his worlds. It is no argument against this theory, that the telescope does not discover it; for the natural eye is made to see natural things, and is no more fitted to see the spiritual than are the nerves of touch to hear music. Another earth might be only ten miles away, and, if the light did not break against it, it would not be visible; and we have no reason to suppose that solar radiation has any relation to spiritual existence; and, if any one supposes that the starry movements would at all interfere with such a world, it may be remembered that the movements of light cross and recross and mingle at ten thousand different angles without any disorder. And also, there is no reason why spirits should be conscious of such motions any more than to-day we feel the swing, sweep, and roll of the earth through space.

V.—THE MATERIAL UNIVERSE STILL OURS.

It does not seem reasonable that we are never to see, or study, or have to do any more with this marvellous handiwork of God's wisdom and power, as displayed in this material cosmos. We live here a few fleeting years, study a little, and wonder at God's work, and then die, knowing not much more of the mysteries of earth than a child knows of his cradle. It can not be that our knowledge is to stop here. No; but from world to world, from system to system, why may we not journey, searching, admiring, adoring the wondrous Maker and our Father at every step? From one room to another in the Father's house we will go, as one who wanders, awed and delighted, from part to part of a glorious cathedral.

We may believe, then, that heaven is made up of the innumerable interstellar rooms that compose the great house of the universe.

I have had, from its very nature, to give considerable space to the answering of this first question, as to the location of heaven. Those that remain are more important, and yet I must compress them into smaller compass. It is hard in one essay to outline a subject that is large enough for a book.

VI.—WHAT IS HEAVEN?

It is not my present purpose to attempt a description of its life or employments. At another time it might not be unprofitable to do this, but not now. What I propose is to unfold the inner and essential principles of heaven. What are the main characteristics of the heavenly existence, that make it heavenly? This I shall try to show.

VII.—HEAVEN IS HARMONY.

The first element of heaven is *harmony*. That which marks the difference between noise and music is that the first is disorder, and the latter is harmony. A discord carried far enough destroys the music, and turns it into noise. The difference between chaos and creation is that one is disorder, and the other harmony again. Break in upon the grand anthem of the stellar movements, and chaos would come again. The difference between health and disease is, once more, just the difference between harmony and disorder. Some disturbing element in the eye, and pain comes, and then blindness; some disturbing element in the blood, and sickness comes, and then, at last, death, or the utter dissolution of the harmony of the body. The only difference between happiness and sorrow, again, is only that between harmony and disorder. What do you mean by being surrounded by pleasant circumstances? Why, this : that you are agreeably related to, in harmony with, your surroundings. What your eye sees, suits you. What your ear hears, suits you. What of odors and fragrance you smell, suits you. What your hands handle, suits you. What your feet fall upon, suits you. That is, you are in harmony with your material conditions. And, as for your social life, the interplay back and forth between you and it is like a piece of perfect mechanism; you are in harmony with society. Let all these conditions exist, and you would be perfectly happy. But, instead of its working like perfect machinery, it breaks and grates and jars continually. Eye is not satisfied, nor ear, nor hand. Plans get broken; families get broken; social ties get broken. And then sin comes into all our lives, and breaks up all harmony of relationship between us and God.

This, then, harmony, is the first and fundamental principle of heaven. In harmony with God, delighting and rejoicing ever in him as your Father; in harmony with all its inhabitants, loving each as yourself, and catching new light from every radiant face; in harmony with the externals of heaven, every sense a luxury and every moment a joy,— these things shall compose the concordant music that shall make all the rooms of the Father's house re-echo with the everlasting joy.

VIII.— HEAVEN IS SATISFACTION.

Another essential element of heaven will be the satisfaction of every desire. Some of the most painful experiences of this life are its unsatisfied longings. What of physical suffering, to one who has felt it, means more than hunger? and the affectional and moral and intellectual tragedies of life are only the histories of its unfed hungers. The hungers of the brain for truths, the hunger of the heart for love, the hunger of the soul for life; the hunger for power, for fame, for pleasure, — these are written all over the face of the earth in fire and tears and blood. How does some desolate, lonely life look back to where some clasped companion hand was wrenched away, and from which hour it has wandered unsatisfied! How does some husband or wife hunger for the unfound ideal that a drunken or faithless mate fails to give them! How do some mother's arms ache with their hunger for the little one gone!

Does it not mean heaven, then, to look up and say, "There I shall be satisfied"? You will not carry all your present wants with you; but every want you do carry will find its answer. And, since we do not now know particularly what all those desires will be, it is proper enough for us to think of heaven as a place where all our present right desires will be satisfied. So if you say to me, "I want this or that in heaven: shall I have it?" I answer unhesitatingly, "Yes." And I say so on this principle: My little boy teases me for something which he wishes me to get him next year. I say, "You may have it;" and yet I may know that, by the time next year has come, he will not want it. I do not falsify: I only accommodate myself to his capacity, and, in a specific instead of a general way, promise him that his desires shall be satisfied.

It is for lack of a little thought in this direction that people have so woefully misunderstood Miss Phelps's little book, "Gates Ajar." Its underlying idea is just common-sense itself. The lady promises the little girl, aching with an unsatisfied musical hunger, and longing to have and play the piano, that she shall have one in heaven. Hungering for cookies, of which her poverty deprives her, she is promised all she wants of them in heaven. And it is simple, common sense. What does she mean? Only this: that her desire for music and her hunger for food should be satisfied. The Bible promises that; and reason teaches that happiness could not exist without it. And, as for the materialism of it, a piano is no more material than a harp, and cookies are just as spiritual as growing apples. And the Apocalypse is full of these not only, but of a hundred other figures quite as sensuous. Satisfaction, then, is the next element of heaven.

IX.—HEAVEN IS EXPANSION.

The life there shall be an expansion. Paul compares the resurrection life to growing grain. At first it is only a single green blade; then it expands and unfolds; it becomes two, then many; it grows, and lifts up; it waves long plumes in the summer air; it buds; it blossoms; it forms young kernels; then fills out its full and heavy head. The process of its whole life is one of expansion. So shall be the eternal life.

Just this is the order of earthly, human life. The new-born babe is a bundle of faculties and powers as yet unrolled. It learns the use of hand and eye and ear; then the mind wakes up, one faculty at a time, curiosity, search, taste, imagination, arrangement, memory, until he expands into merchant, artist, statesman, orator. But every man feels that he has wings in him not yet unfolded, that he has a thousand capabilities not yet explored. The air of heaven shall open them as a June day unfolds a flower.

We may have in heaven, — and parables like that of the talents strongly indicate it, — the gradual development of whole sets of faculties as yet unimagined. Fœtal life could never dream out this earth-life. The caterpillar could never imagine himself a butterfly.

We may have more than five senses there. Why not fifty? God will give us keys to every room in his house. We have no reason to assume that there are only five, because we have as yet the use of only five. We know now there are lights we cannot see, and heats we cannot feel, and sounds we cannot hear. Why not other things that are neither of these, and the nature of which is at present unknown?

Heavenly life will be expansive life. Each new day — or what stands for days in heaven — shall find us more and greater than we were; and so on forever.

X.—HEAVEN IS PROGRESS.

And lastly, on this point, the heaven-life will be one of progress.

God has made it one of the essential characteristics of man, that he should always press on to seek what lies beyond. This is the secret of scientific advance. The universe is like a house with all its rooms locked. Man works till he opens one door; and, after gazing for a little at the new wonders, he attacks another lock, and pushes back its wards; and so from room he presses on to room. Through years of toil, by sea and land, he has worked, to open up to light the surface of the earth; and still to-day the workers toil. Livingstone plunges into Central Africa, after the Nile fountain and other secrets; and ship after ship still knocks for admission at the icy gates of the Polar Sea. All are impelled by the desire to know. A hundred earth-born sciences illustrate the same truth; and beyond earth, through ages of labor, mankind has pushed out his adventurous voyages of discovery among the stars. And this work has just begun. This search for what is beyond, I say, is a characteristic of the race. Nothing more to discover, to conquer, to do, is only to say that misery has come down on human life. From the restless, idle boy, to retired merchants, old men beyond their work, and Alexanders with no more worlds to conquer, stagnation is misery and sorrow. And there is nothing in death to change all this.

Once imagine heaven to have nothing **more** to learn or to do, and the cup of **eternal** life would have reached its bitter dregs, instead of **proving an** exhaustless **fountain.** The songs would die down, the harps grow silent, and all creatures long for an oblivious **sleep.**

And so **just this** eternal progress that the soul demands finds its reason in the fact that God **is** infinite and unsearchable, and we are his finite children. Just as one might climb a mountain, and get no nearer the moon; or sail the sea forever, with his eye upon, but never overtaking, **a star,** — **so we** will climb up ever into new heights of the beauty and glory and love of God, but never find the end.

O, the life of heaven! We think it strange **that it** is covered with mystery; but well has God thus covered **it.** Did it lie open to us, we should **be sick** with longing, and so **unfit** for our work and discipline. Could the world catch **its** music, and **see its** glories, **we** should wish for the knife or the poison that **even** with violence should open **for us a** way through the closed doors of our fleshly tabernacles.

> "We speak of the realms of the blest,
>   That country so bright and so fair,
> . And oft are its glories confest;
>   But what must it be to be there?"

XI. — TERMS OF ADMISSION.

It only remains for me now to indicate the terms **of** admission. We all wish to enter heaven; and God grant we may! But how? "Tell me the way to this blessed country, for I fain would become a pilgrim thither," I hear you say. "Who shall ascend into the hill of the Lord, and who shall stand in his holy place?" Listen to the answer. "He that hath clean hands and a pure heart." You have the answer; but let me unfold it a little, and put it into other language.

The whole secret is just here. In order to enter, you must have ability to see heaven, to hear it, and to feel it. Man's happiness comes not from where he is, what he has, nor what surrounds him; but from his capacity to use and appropriate to his own enjoyment. Two men may take a walk together: one knows botany, geology, mineralogy, chemistry, natural history, etc.; the other, none of them. The latter finds his walk exceedingly dull, and he does not see any thing to amuse or instruct; but every flower, every stone, the insects in the air, and the squirrel in the wall, speak to the other, and fill him with wonder and delight at the wondrous works of God. Now, in the external sense of having, one man has just as much as the other; but one is capable of appreciating it all, and the other none. Take a blind man up the monument on Bunker Hill: talk of the city at his feet, and of the western hills glorious with sunset; point out the river sweeping peacefully by, the harbor beyond, and the ocean that bounds it; then talk of sister cities set round like precious stones about a central gem; but he is blind, and you only mock and torture him with

Heaven.

delights he knows of, but cannot share. Invite a deaf friend to go and hear Albani with you: let him see her come upon the stage, and from her parted lips pour out the invisible melody of song: it is torment to him. The music is all around him. O, if only for one moment he could hear! **And so the key to heaven is the ability to enjoy it.** Unless you have in you the awakening and culture of your spiritual faculties, you may be under the very shadow of the throne, and never **know** it; its music may roll all about you, and you never know it; its airs may fan your cheeks, and you never know it; its celestial scenery may stretch out, — fair vales, and mighty hills, and gentle streams, and fadeless trees, — and you never know it. As one might sleep in the central bower of a garden, all the beauties and sweets close around him, **and** yet he be suffering in awful dreams, and tortured with a thousand terrors, you may be the central one in the throng of the blest; and yet, unless in your own soul you are spiritually alive, it may be to you only the lowest abyss of hell. Fitness for heaven, then, is the key to it.

PROGRESS.

THEY'LL not stand still in that summer land:
   The baby whose tiny feet
Went climbing the ladder where angels stand
   A baby no more you'll greet.

A strong young man, or a maiden fair,
   In the Father's house to-day
Is the little one of the sunny hair,
   That prattled about your way.

O, tell me, then, is the baby lost?
   Would you have the baby face
Forever smooth, with no thought-lines crost,
   For the sake of the baby grace?

My darling is too dear to me
   To wish it so much of ill:
Let the loved one grow in eternity,
   But stay my darling still.

Progress.

However great the blest may grow,
　　However they out-tower
The thought and the life we lead below,
　　There never will come an hour

When they will forget us; for grandest souls
　　Are grandest still in this:
As the endless scroll of heaven unrolls
　　Its mystery of bliss, —

They do not lose their thought of those
　　They loved in days gone by;
For the spirit, the nearer God it grows,
　　Loves thee more tenderly.

The higher in heaven my loved ones rise,
　　The lower still they bend;
And ages of progress in the skies
　　Hold for me still my friend.

A. R. C.

WHEN falls the night upon the earth,
   And all in shadow lies,
The sun's not dead: his radiance still
   Beams bright on other skies.

And when the morning star fades out,
   On the pale brow of dawn,
Though lost a while to earthly eyes,
   It still keeps shining on.

Some other world is glad to see
   Our star that's gone away:
The light whose going makes our night
   Makes somewhere else a day.

The feet that cease their walking here,
   Grown weary of earth's road,
With tireless strength go travelling
   The pathway up to God.

A. R. C.

The hands whose patient fingers now
    Have laid earth's labors by,
With loving skill have taken up
    Some higher ministry.

The eyes that give no longer back
    The tender look of love,
Now, with a deathless gleam, drink in
    God's beauteous world above.

The lips whose sweet tones made us ask
    If angels sweeter sung,
Though silent here, make heaven glad
    With their melodious tongue.

And, though her body lies asleep,
    Our favorite is not dead:
She rises from dark death's bright birth
    "With joy upon her head."

And she is just our loved one still,
    And loves us now no less:
She goes away to come again, —
    To watch us, and to bless.

And though we cannot clasp her hand,
    Nor look upon her face,
Nor listen to her voice again,
    Nor watch her ways of grace, —

Light on the Cloud.

Still we can keep her memory bright,
    And walk the way she trod,
And know she waits until we come
    Up to the house of God.

Let us be thankful, through our tears,
    That she was ours so long,
And try to lift our tones of grief
    T' accord with her heaven song.

www.ingramcontent.com/pod-product-compliance
Lightning Source LLC
Chambersburg PA
CBHW022111160426
43197CB00009B/983